SLOW COOKER VEGETARIAN

SLOW COOKER VEGETARIAN

HEALTHY AND WHOLESOME, COMFORTING AND CONVENIENT

KATY HOLDER

MURDOCH BOOKS

SYDNEY · LONDON

Contents

Introduction

Whether you've been using a slow cooker for years or have just bought your first one, this collection of vegetarian dishes is a great place to start or continue your journey. Quite often people think of slow cookers as useful pieces of equipment for cooking tough cuts of meat. However, they are equally fantastic for vegetables, allowing you to cook them gently and slowly until they are wonderfully tender and juicy – or still firm, depending on the desired result.

The joy of prepping and forgetting

Due to the high water content of vegetables, it's important not to cook them for hours and hours. So, rather than using the traditional 'leave for eight hours while you go to work' approach, many of the recipes in this book are cooked for just three or four hours. The beauty of this timeline is that you can do some preparation, throw everything in the slow cooker, do the washing up and then have a few free hours to read stories to your kids, help them with homework, go for a walk, run errands and so on. Best of all, after dinner, there is often only one pot to wash up!

One point to remember when using a slow cooker is that, unlike cooking in an oven or on the stovetop, liquid is unable to evaporate, so it's important to add much less liquid than you normally would. Don't worry if when you start your dish it looks dry. By the end of the cooking time, the vegetables will be cooked and (if intended) saucy.

Cooking for the family

Slow cookers are ideal for cooking healthy meals for your family because you start with predominantly fresh, whole foods and very few nutrients are lost in the cooking process. Slow cookers work differently than, say, boiling vegetables in a saucepan, as they retain all of the vegetables' natural juices in the sauce, resulting in a richly flavoured, nutrient-dense dish.

The recipes in this book are all vegetarian, but this doesn't mean they use only vegetables. Many provide a complete balanced meal, including vegetables, beans and pulses, with no need for additional protein. When cooking pantry staples like pulses and beans, dried and tinned versions work equally well. Just ensure that if you are using dried pulses and beans, you soak and pre-cook as required beforehand. Slow cookers are also ideal for cooking rice and you will find plenty of recipes in this book for rice dishes, such as risotto and paella.

If you'd like to offer options, or introduce new flavours to kids and fussy adult eaters, this book offers topping ideas that can be used to add even more flavour or texture to many of the dishes. Put them in the middle of the table when the meal is served and let everyone choose their own. For many kids, herbs, chilli and citrus can take a bit of time to get used to, so adding them as toppings introduces these flavours slowly. The seed crunch topping on page 9 not only adds crunch, but extra protein and healthy fats, too.

And speaking of cooking for the family, we've also included desserts! When cooking desserts, keep a close eye to ensure your recipe doesn't overcook, as the size of the slow cooker can affect some of the puddings. Keep watch through the lid, resisting the temptation to keep lifting it up and letting the heat escape. When your dessert is finished, remove the lid quickly so the condensation doesn't drip onto your delicious pudding.

Slow cookers are often thought of as convenient for the cooler months. However, I like to use them in the warmer months, too, as they don't heat up the house like a stovetop or oven. The warm salad recipes in particular are great for summer lunches or dinner parties. Get them cooking early on, then concentrate on other aspects of your meal. Leave the salads to cool and then enjoy your feast.

Let's get started

This book is divided into chapters with recipes for soups; dals and curries; family favourites; rice, pasta and grains; warm salads and sides and of course scrumptious desserts. Since everyone's slow cooker is different, most of the recipes do not require any particular size and have been tested in many different sized cookers. Your slow cooker will probably work best when it is between half and two-thirds full.

There isn't much you can't do in a slow cooker. So dig yours out from the back of your cupboard – or buy one next time you are shopping – and reclaim your precious time!

SLOW COOKER TIPS

✔ Most slow cookers are very simple to operate with low, high and auto settings (or 1, 2 and auto), but read the instruction manual for your particular slow cooker before starting to cook.

✔ Some slow cookers have an insert pan that can be used on a stovetop and then put back to continue cooking. Many of the recipes in this book suggest frying off some ingredients before cooking in the slow cooker. If your slow cooker's insert pan can be used on the stovetop, then do all the cooking in the pan; if not, use a frying pan. The majority of ceramic insert pans cannot be used on your stovetop and will crack. Refer to the instruction manual to see if yours is suitable.

✘ If you have put your slow cooker's ceramic insert in the fridge for any reason before cooking, allow it to come to room temperature before starting to cook or it may crack once it starts heating up, due to the sudden change in temperature.

✘ Never cook dried kidney beans and other kidney-shaped beans from raw in a slow cooker because the temperature isn't high enough to destroy the natural toxins found in these beans. Always soak them overnight and then boil for 10 minutes before adding. It's fine to add drained and rinsed tinned beans straight into the cooker.

Toppings

Pangrattato
(garlic and herb breadcrumbs)

1 tablespoon olive oil

30 g (1 oz/½ cup) panko breadcrumbs

1 small garlic clove, crushed

finely grated zest of 1 lemon

1 tablespoon finely chopped flat-leaf (Italian) parsley
  or basil

Heat the oil in a large frying pan over medium–high
heat. Add the breadcrumbs and cook, tossing the pan
regularly for 4–5 minutes until the breadcrumbs are
lightly golden. Add the garlic and a pinch of sea salt
and cook for 1 minute more. Remove from the pan and
stir in the lemon zest and your choice of herb.

Lemon and dill yoghurt

150 g (5½ oz) Greek-style yoghurt

1 teaspoon finely grated lemon zest

2 teaspoons lemon juice

1 tablespoon finely chopped dill

Combine all the ingredients in a small bowl with a little
sea salt and freshly ground black pepper.

Chilli and herb oil

80 ml (2½ fl oz/⅓ cup) extra virgin olive oil

1 red bird's eye or long red chilli, thinly sliced

basil leaves, coarsely torn or 2 tablespoons finely chopped flat-leaf (Italian) parsley

Combine all the ingredients in a small bowl, season with sea salt and freshly ground black pepper and use as a drizzle at the table.

If you love spice, use a bird's eye chilli. Otherwise use a long red chilli, which tends to be milder.

Seed crunch

35 g (1¼ oz/¼ cup) pepitas (pumpkin seeds)

35 g (1¼ oz/¼ cup) slivered almonds

3 teaspoons chia seeds

2 teaspoons white sesame seeds

Put all the ingredients into a large cold frying pan over medium heat. Cook, tossing regularly for 3–4 minutes until lightly golden and toasted. Cool before serving.

This seed mix can be stored in an airtight container for a couple of weeks, so make a larger quantity for scattering over soups, stews and salads.

Gremolata

small handful flat-leaf (Italian) parsley leaves,
  finely chopped
1 garlic clove, crushed or finely chopped
2 teaspoons finely grated lemon zest

Combine all the ingredients in a small bowl and
season with sea salt and freshly ground black pepper.
Although not traditional, a drizzle of olive oil can
also be added.

Cucumber raita

½ Lebanese (short) cucumber
150 g (5½ oz) Greek-style yoghurt
½ small garlic clove, crushed
2 teaspoons finely chopped mint

Cut the cucumber in half lengthways and scrape out
the seeds using a teaspoon. Finely dice the flesh and
combine with the yoghurt, garlic and mint and season
with a pinch of sea salt.

Feta and red chilli crumble

100 g (3½ oz) feta cheese, crumbled
1 long red chilli, seeds removed, finely chopped
1 teaspoon dried oregano

Gently combine all the ingredients in a bowl and season with pepper (the feta is salty). Scatter over dishes as desired.

Salsa verde

handful coarsely chopped mint leaves
handful coarsely chopped basil leaves
large handful coarsely chopped flat-leaf (Italian) parsley leaves
1 tablespoon finely chopped capers
2 tablespoons extra virgin olive oil
2 tablespoons lemon juice

Process all the ingredients in a small food processor. Alternatively, finely chop the herbs and capers and combine with the oil and lemon juice.

SOUPS

PUMPKIN SOUP WITH A TWIST! THIS CLASSIC SOUP GETS A DELICIOUS MAKE-OVER WITH THE ADDITION OF AROMATIC THAI FLAVOURS: LIME LEAVES, LEMONGRASS AND LIME JUICE.

Thai-style pumpkin soup

SERVES 4–6
PREPARATION TIME 25 MINUTES
COOKING TIME 3 HOURS

2 butternut pumpkins (squash), about 3 kg (6 lb 12 oz) peeled, seeded and chopped

1 brown onion, finely chopped

2 kaffir lime leaves, torn

1 lemongrass stem, bruised

1 teaspoon finely grated fresh ginger

2 teaspoons soy sauce

270 ml (9½ fl oz) tin coconut cream

1 tablespoon mild Thai red curry paste

875 ml (30 fl oz/3½ cups) good-quality vegetable stock

2 teaspoons lime juice

2 tablespoons Thai sweet chilli sauce

coriander (cilantro) leaves, to garnish

1 long red chilli, thinly sliced

Put the pumpkin and onion into a slow cooker with the lime leaves, lemongrass, ginger and soy sauce.

Reserve 2 tablespoons of the coconut cream, then mix the curry paste with the remaining coconut cream until smooth. Pour over the pumpkin mixture, then pour in the stock and gently mix together.

Cover and cook on high for 3 hours, or until the pumpkin is tender. Set aside to cool slightly. Remove the lime leaves and lemongrass stem.

Purée the mixture until smooth, using a stick blender, food processor or blender. Stir in the lime juice and sweet chilli sauce.

Ladle into bowls and drizzle with the reserved coconut cream. Serve garnished with the coriander and chilli.

TIP This soup can be frozen. Allow the soup to cool, then transfer to an airtight container. Label and date the container and freeze for up to 6 months.

A STRIKINGLY COLOURED, VELVETY SOUP THAT TASTES EVERY BIT AS GOOD AS IT LOOKS. SERVE THIS THE RUSSIAN WAY WITH RYE CROUTONS, SOUR CREAM AND DILL.

Borscht

SERVES 4–6
PREPARATION TIME 10 MINUTES
COOKING TIME 7 HOURS

1 kg (2 lb 4 oz) beetroot (beets), peeled and cut into 3 cm (1¼ inch) pieces

1 brown onion, finely chopped

1.5 litres (52 fl oz/6 cups) good-quality vegetable stock

400 g (14 oz) potatoes, peeled and coarsely chopped

3 tablespoons finely chopped dill stems

1 fresh or dried bay leaf

dill sprigs and sour cream or crème fraîche, to serve

Rye croutons

6 slices rye bread

2 tablespoons olive oil

sea salt

Put the beetroot, onion, stock, potatoes, dill stems and bay leaf into the slow cooker. Season with sea salt and freshly ground black pepper, then cook on high for 7 hours, or until the beetroot is tender.

When the soup has about 30 minutes to go, make the rye croutons. Heat the oven to 190°C (375°F). Cut the bread into 1–2 cm (½–¾ inch) cubes, leaving the crusts on. Put in a large bowl, add the olive oil and season with salt. Toss to coat in the oil. Arrange in a single layer on a baking tray and bake for about 15 minutes, turning every 5 minutes, until crisp.

Remove the bay leaf from the soup and discard. Using a stick blender, food processor or blender, purée the soup in batches until smooth. Check the seasoning.

Serve with the rye croutons, dill sprigs and sour cream or crème fraîche.

SPICED, NOT SPICY. WITH A HINT OF CUMIN AND SOME FRESH GINGER JUICE ADDED AT THE END, THIS SOUP SHOULD STILL BE A HIT WITH THE WHOLE FAMILY.

Spiced carrot and cumin soup

SERVES 4
PREPARATION TIME 20 MINUTES
COOKING TIME 6 HOURS 10 MINUTES

1 tablespoon vegetable oil

1 brown onion, chopped

2 garlic cloves, chopped

1 kg (2 lb 4 oz) carrots, halved lengthways and cut into 1 cm (½ inch) pieces

1 potato, peeled and cut into 2 cm (¾ inch) chunks

3 teaspoons ground cumin

1 teaspoon ground coriander

1 teaspoon sea salt

375 ml (13 fl oz/1½ cups) good-quality vegetable stock

2 teaspoons honey

5 cm (2 inch) piece of fresh ginger, peeled

3–4 tablespoons shredded mint

Heat the oil in the insert pan of a slow cooker or a frying pan over medium heat. Add the onion, garlic, carrot and potato and cook for 10 minutes, or until the vegetables have softened, stirring occasionally. Add the spices and salt and cook for 1 minute.

Return the insert pan, if using, to the slow cooker, or transfer the vegetable mixture to the slow cooker. Add the stock, honey and 125 ml (4 fl oz/½ cup) water. Season well with freshly ground black pepper and stir to combine. Cover and cook on low for 6 hours, or until the carrot is very tender.

Purée the mixture until smooth, using a stick blender, food processor or blender. Finely grate the ginger, then squeeze it over a small bowl to extract the juice. Stir the ginger juice through the soup, then season to taste.

Ladle into bowls and serve with the mint scattered on top.

CASHEWS GIVE THIS VEGAN SOUP THE SORT OF VELVETY CREAMINESS YOU'D USUALLY ASSOCIATE WITH CREAM OR BUTTER, AND THE ANISEED FLAVOUR OF FENNEL MARRIES WELL WITH THE EARTHINESS OF THE POTATOES.

Leek, fennel and potato soup with herb salsa

SERVES 4–6
PREPARATION TIME 10 MINUTES
COOKING TIME 5 HOURS

60 ml (2 fl oz/¼ cup) extra virgin olive oil

3 leeks, white part only, washed, thinly sliced

2 garlic cloves, coarsely chopped

1 fennel bulb, halved, thinly sliced

800 g (1 lb 12 oz) potatoes, cut into 4 cm (1½ inch) pieces

1.5 litres (52 fl oz/6 cups) good-quality vegetable stock

50 g (1¾ oz/⅓ cup) raw cashews

2 teaspoons fennel seeds, toasted, coarsely ground

crusty bread, to serve

Herb salsa

large handful flat-leaf (Italian) parsley, coarsely chopped

3–4 tablespoons coarsely chopped mint

1 tablespoon finely snipped chives

finely grated zest of 1 lemon

80 ml (2½ fl oz/⅓ cup) extra virgin olive oil, plus extra for drizzling

Put all the soup ingredients into the slow cooker and season with sea salt and freshly ground black pepper. Cook on high for 5 hours, or until all the vegetables are tender.

When the soup has 10 minutes left to cook, put the herb salsa ingredients in a bowl and mix to combine well.

Using a stick blender, food processor or blender, purée the soup in batches until smooth, then check the seasoning. Serve with the salsa and crusty bread.

TIP If you don't want to make the herb salsa, simply scatter some chopped herbs over the soup before serving.

KORMA CURRY POWDERS ARE MILDER THAN MANY OTHER
INDIAN SPICE MIXES, SO THIS IS A GREAT WAY TO INTRODUCE
AROMATIC FOOD TO YOUR FAMILY. ADD LESS IF YOUR FAMILY IS
STILL GETTING USED TO SPICINESS.

Indian curried yellow split pea and coconut soup

SERVES 6–8
PREPARATION TIME 20 MINUTES
COOKING TIME 3 HOURS 40 MINUTES

2 tablespoons olive oil

2 brown onions, finely diced

3 garlic cloves, thinly sliced

1 leek, white part only, washed, thinly sliced

1 carrot, diced

1–3 tablespoons korma curry powder

660 g (1 lb 7 oz/3 cups) yellow split peas, rinsed

2 litres (70 fl oz/8 cups) good-quality
    vegetable stock

300 ml (10½ fl oz) coconut milk

45 g (1½ oz/1 cup) baby spinach leaves

juice of 2 limes, or to taste

1 long red chilli, thinly sliced diagonally,
    Greek-style yoghurt and coriander (cilantro)
    leaves, to serve

Heat the olive oil in the insert pan of a slow cooker or a frying pan over medium heat. Add the onion, garlic, leek and carrot and sauté for 5–7 minutes, or until tender. Add the curry powder and stir for 30 seconds, or until aromatic.

Return the insert pan, if using, to the slow cooker, or transfer the vegetable mixture to the slow cooker. Add the split peas and stock. Cover and cook on high for 3½ hours, or until the split peas are very tender.

Stir the coconut milk through. Purée the mixture to a rough consistency, using a stick blender, food processor or blender, leaving some of the soup un-puréed if desired. (You may need to add a little extra coconut milk to reach your desired consistency.) Stir in the spinach and lime juice, to taste. Season with sea salt and freshly ground black pepper.

Ladle into bowls and serve topped with chilli, yoghurt and coriander.

THIS SOUP USES DRIED BEANS, WHICH MUST BE SOAKED FOR AT LEAST 8 HOURS OR OVERNIGHT BEFORE THE SOUP CAN BE COOKED. RIBOLLITA IS A TRADITIONAL HEARTY TUSCAN SOUP THAT INCLUDES BREAD AND GREEN VEGETABLES.

Ribollita

SERVES 7–8
PREPARATION TIME 25 MINUTES (+ 8 HOURS SOAKING)
COOKING TIME 6 HOURS 20 MINUTES

150 g (5½ oz/¾ cup) dried cannellini beans

2 tablespoons olive oil

1 large brown onion, chopped

2 carrots, cut into 1 cm (½ inch) dice

3 celery stalks, cut into 1 cm (½ inch) dice

3 garlic cloves, chopped

400 g (14 oz) tin chopped tomatoes

1 tablespoon thyme leaves

650 g (1 lb 7 oz) large waxy potatoes, peeled and cut into 1.5 cm (⅝ inch) dice

175 g (6 oz) cavolo nero (black kale), trimmed and coarsely shredded (see Tip)

1 loaf of rustic bread, such as ciabatta or sourdough, thickly sliced

finely grated parmesan cheese, to serve

extra virgin olive oil, for drizzling

Soak the beans for 8 hours or overnight in plenty of cold water. Drain the beans, discarding the water, then place in a large saucepan. Cover with fresh water and bring to the boil. Boil rapidly for 10 minutes. Rinse the beans and drain again.

Heat the olive oil in the insert pan of a slow cooker or a large frying pan over low heat. Add the onion, carrot and celery and cook for 8 minutes, or until softened, stirring occasionally. Add the garlic and cook for 2 minutes, stirring frequently.

Return the insert pan, if using, to the slow cooker, or transfer the vegetable mixture to the slow cooker. Add the beans, tomatoes, thyme, potato and 2 litres (70 fl oz/8 cups) of water. Cover and cook on low for 5 hours, or until the beans and potato are nearly tender.

Stir the cavolo nero through the soup. Cover, increase the heat to high and cook for a further 1 hour. Season to taste with sea salt and freshly ground black pepper.

Tear the bread slices into chunks and place in bowls. Ladle the soup over the top. Sprinkle with parmesan and some more black pepper, drizzle with extra virgin olive oil and serve.

TIP Instead of cavolo nero (also called Tuscan black cabbage or Tuscan kale), you can use kale or silverbeet (Swiss chard) if desired. If using kale, strip the leaves from the stalks.

FOR THIS VELVETY SOUP, YOU CAN USE ANY WHITE BEANS THAT ARE
ROUGHLY THE SAME SIZE AS CANNELLINI BEANS, SUCH AS HARICOT OR GREAT
NORTHERN – JUST DON'T FORGET TO SOAK THEM OVERNIGHT. CELERIAC
MAKES A GREAT WINTER-TIME SUBSTITUTE FOR THE CAULIFLOWER.

Cauliflower and cannellini bean soup with crispy sage

SERVES 4
PREPARATION TIME 5 MINUTES (+ OVERNIGHT SOAKING)
COOKING TIME 4½ HOURS

2 tablespoons olive oil

2 garlic cloves, coarsely chopped

1 brown onion, finely chopped

1 large leek, white part only, washed, chopped

200 g (7 oz/1 cup) dried cannellini beans, soaked overnight, drained and rinsed

1 small cauliflower, broken into florets, stem thickly sliced

1.25 litres (44 fl oz/5 cups) good-quality vegetable stock

handful sage leaves

extra virgin olive oil, to drizzle (optional)

Heat 1 tablespoon of the oil in a large, heavy-based saucepan over medium–high heat and cook the garlic, onion and leek for 5 minutes or until lightly golden. Add the beans and 375 ml (13 fl oz/1½ cups) of water. Bring to the boil and cook for 20 minutes, then transfer to the slow cooker, along with the cauliflower and stock. Cook on high for 4 hours, or until the cauliflower and beans are tender.

Using a stick blender, food processor or blender, purée the soup until smooth. Check the seasoning, and if necessary season with sea salt and freshly ground black pepper.

Heat the remaining tablespoon of oil in a frying pan over medium–high heat and cook the sage leaves for 2 minutes until crisp. Drain on paper towel. Serve the soup topped with the crispy sage and a drizzle of extra virgin olive oil, if you like.

Cream of mushroom soup

SERVES 4
PREPARATION TIME 20 MINUTES (+ 20 MINUTES SOAKING)
COOKING TIME 2 HOURS 5 MINUTES

10 g (¼ oz) dried porcini mushrooms

1 leek, white part only, washed, thinly sliced

200 g (7 oz) Swiss brown mushrooms, coarsely
  chopped

300 g (10½ oz) large mushroom flats, coarsely
  chopped

125 ml (4 fl oz/½ cup) Madeira (see Tip)

1 litre (35 fl oz/4 cups) good-quality vegetable
  stock

2 teaspoons chopped marjoram, plus extra
  leaves, to garnish

85 g (3 oz/⅓ cup) sour cream or crème fraîche

crusty bread, to serve

Soak the porcini mushrooms in 250 ml (9 fl oz/1 cup) of boiling water for 20 minutes. Using a slotted spoon, remove the mushrooms from the soaking liquid and put into the slow cooker. Pour the soaking liquid through a fine-mesh sieve into a jug, to remove any impurities.

Add the strained soaking liquid to the slow cooker with the leek, Swiss brown mushrooms and mushroom flats, Madeira, stock and half the chopped marjoram. Season to taste with sea salt and freshly ground black pepper. Cover and cook on high for 2 hours.

Purée the mixture until smooth, using a stick blender, food processor or blender. Stir the sour cream through and cook for a further 5 minutes. Stir in the remaining chopped marjoram.

Check seasoning, then ladle into bowls, garnish with marjoram leaves and serve with crusty bread.

TIP Madeira is a fortified wine made in Portugal. Malmsey is the richest and fruitiest of the Madeiras and can also be enjoyed as an after-dinner drink. If unavailable, use sherry.

WITH THIS BEAUTIFULLY THICK AND CREAMY BEAN SOUP, VEGANS
NEED NOT MISS OUT ON THE SIMPLE PLEASURES OF A COMFORTING
BOWL OF SOUP ON A COLD WINTER'S NIGHT.

Moroccan broad bean soup

SERVES 6
PREPARATION TIME 20 MINUTES (+ OVERNIGHT SOAKING)
COOKING TIME 3¼ HOURS

570 g (1 lb 4½ oz/3 cups) dried broad beans, soaked overnight, drained and rinsed

2 tablespoons olive oil

1 large brown onion, chopped

4 garlic cloves, crushed or finely chopped

1 teaspoon ground cumin

1 teaspoon ground coriander

½ teaspoon sweet paprika

500 ml (17 fl oz/2 cups) good-quality vegetable stock

1 large potato, peeled, cut into large pieces

finely grated zest and juice of 1 lemon

chopped coriander (cilantro), paprika and extra virgin olive oil, to serve

Remove the skins from the soaked broad beans.

Heat the oil in a large saucepan over medium heat. Add the onion, garlic and spices and cook for 3–5 minutes until the onion has softened slightly. Add the beans and 1 litre (35 fl oz/4 cups) of water and bring to the boil. Cook for 10 minutes, then transfer to the slow cooker, along with the stock and potato. Cook on high for 3 hours, or until the beans and potato are tender.

Using a stick blender, food processor or blender, purée the soup in batches until smooth, adding the lemon juice and zest, plus a little water if the soup is too thick.

Season to taste with sea salt and freshly ground black pepper, then serve with coriander, paprika and a drizzle of extra virgin olive oil.

Cream of parsnip soup

SERVES 4–6
PREPARATION TIME 20 MINUTES
COOKING TIME 4 HOURS 20 MINUTES

1 kg (2 lb 4 oz) parsnips, peeled and chopped

200 g (7 oz) all-purpose potatoes, such as sebago, peeled and chopped

1 granny smith apple, peeled, cored and chopped

1 brown onion, finely chopped

1 garlic clove, chopped

750 ml (26 fl oz/3 cups) good-quality vegetable stock

pinch of saffron threads

250 ml (9 fl oz/1 cup) thin (pouring) cream

snipped chives, to serve

Place the parsnip and potato in the slow cooker with the apple, onion and garlic. Stir in the stock and saffron threads. Cover and cook on high for 4 hours.

Purée the mixture until smooth, using a stick blender, food processor or blender. Season to taste with sea salt, then stir in the cream. Cover and cook for a further 20 minutes.

Ladle into bowls and serve sprinkled with chives and plenty of freshly ground black pepper.

ANY ORANGE-FLESHED PUMPKIN, SUCH AS BUTTERNUT, WORKS WELL
IN THIS SOOTHING AND NOURISHING SOUP. IF YOU CAN'T FIND
LEMON THYME, JUST USE REGULAR THYME.

Pumpkin and red lentil soup

SERVES 4–6
PREPARATION TIME 15 MINUTES
COOKING TIME 4 HOURS

1 tablespoon olive oil

20 g (¾ oz) butter

1 brown onion, coarsely chopped

2 garlic cloves, crushed or finely chopped

½ teaspoon chilli powder

¼ teaspoon ground nutmeg

1 fresh or dried bay leaf

4 lemon thyme sprigs, leaves picked

1.2 kg (2 lb 12 oz) pumpkin (winter squash), seeds removed, peeled, cut into 3 cm (1¼ inch) cubes

200 g (7 oz/1 cup) red lentils, rinsed

1 litre (35 fl oz/4 cups) good-quality vegetable stock

Greek-style yoghurt and toasted pepitas (pumpkin seeds), to serve

Heat the oil and butter in the insert pan of a slow cooker or a frying pan over medium heat. Cook the onion for 3 minutes until slightly softened, then add the garlic, chilli, nutmeg, bay leaf and thyme and cook for a further 2 minutes until fragrant.

Return the insert pan, if using, to the slow cooker, or transfer the mixture to the slow cooker, along with the pumpkin, lentils, stock and 250 ml (9 fl oz/1 cup) of water. Season with sea salt and freshly ground black pepper, then cook on high for 4 hours, or until the pumpkin and lentils are tender.

Using a stick blender, food processor or blender, purée the soup until smooth. Check the seasoning, then serve with yoghurt and toasted pepitas.

THIS SOUP IS BEST MADE AT THE HEIGHT OF SUMMER WHEN TOMATOES ARE AT THEIR RIPEST AND MOST FLAVOURSOME.

Herbed tomato soup with garlic toasts

SERVES 6
PREPARATION TIME 20 MINUTES
COOKING TIME 6 HOURS

2 kg (4 lb 8 oz) mixed tomatoes (see Tip)

small handful flat-leaf (Italian) parsley leaves, chopped

small handful whole basil leaves

2 tablespoons fresh oregano leaves

5 garlic cloves, peeled and halved

1 long red chilli, halved lengthways

1 red onion, cut into wedges

1 dried bay leaf

375 ml (13 fl oz/1½ cups) tomato juice

1½ tablespoons brown sugar

1 tablespoon red wine vinegar or sherry vinegar

1 teaspoon sea salt

½ teaspoon freshly ground black pepper

80 ml (2½ fl oz/⅓ cup) olive oil

4 thick sourdough bread slices

Using a sharp knife, cut a cross in the base of each tomato, except for any cherry tomatoes. Working in batches, blanch the tomatoes in boiling water for 30 seconds, until their skins loosen. Drain the tomatoes and leave until cool enough to handle, then peel the skins away from the cross. Cut each tomato into quarters and remove the core.

Arrange the fresh herbs in a slow cooker. Scatter eight of the garlic clove halves, the chilli and onion over the top, then top with the tomatoes and bay leaf.

Mix together the tomato juice, sugar, vinegar, salt, pepper and 60 ml (2 fl oz/¼ cup) of the olive oil, then pour over the tomatoes. Cover and cook on low for 6 hours, or until the onion is very soft. Remove the bay leaf.

Purée the mixture to a rough consistency, using a stick blender, food processor or blender.

Brush the bread slices with the remaining olive oil and chargrill for 2 minutes on each side. Rub with the remaining garlic clove halves and serve with the soup.

TIP Use whatever tomatoes are in season and are at their ripest. If you use any cherry tomatoes, there is no need to peel them.

Sweet potato and carrot soup with cheesy agnolotti

SERVES 4
PREPARATION TIME 20 MINUTES
COOKING TIME 3¼ HOURS

1 tablespoon olive oil

2 garlic cloves, crushed or finely chopped

1 red onion, finely chopped

800 g (1 lb 12 oz) sweet potato, peeled, cut into 2 cm (¾ inch) pieces

3 carrots, cut into 1 cm (½ inch) slices

1 litre (35 fl oz/4 cups) good-quality vegetable stock

6 thyme sprigs, tied together with kitchen string

150 g (5½ oz) feta cheese, crumbled

150 g (5½ oz) bocconcini, coarsely chopped

20 dumpling wrappers

mint leaves, to serve

Heat the oil in the insert pan of a slow cooker or a large saucepan over medium heat. Cook the garlic and onion for 5 minutes until softened. Return the insert pan, if using, to the slow cooker, or transfer the mixture to the slow cooker, along with the sweet potato, carrot, stock, thyme and 250 ml (9 fl oz/1 cup) of water. Cook on high for 3 hours, or until the vegetables are very tender. Remove the thyme and discard.

Meanwhile, combine the cheeses in a bowl. To make the filled pasta, or agnolotti, place 2 teaspoons of the cheese filling onto one half of each dumpling wrapper. Wet your hands and run a fingertip around the edge of the wrappers, then fold to enclose the filling, ensuring there are no air pockets. Press along the edges with the back of a fork to seal.

Bring a large saucepan of salted water to the boil. Cook the agnolotti for 2 minutes until they float to the surface, then drain.

Remove one-third of the soup and purée with a stick blender, food processor or blender until smooth. Return to the slow cooker, along with the agnolotti, and cook for about 5 minutes until warmed through.

Season the soup with sea salt and freshly ground black pepper, then serve with mint leaves.

CANNELLINI BEANS ARE IDEAL IN WINTER SOUPS FOR THEIR CREAMY TEXTURE. THEY HAVE A MILD FLAVOUR, SO FOR AN ADDED BOOST SWIRL IN A DOLLOP OF HOMEMADE PESTO JUST BEFORE SERVING.

White bean and rocket soup with basil pesto

SERVES 6
PREPARATION TIME 15 MINUTES
COOKING TIME 8 HOURS 20 MINUTES

1 large brown onion, chopped

2 garlic cloves, crushed

2 x 400 g (14 oz) tins cannellini beans, drained and rinsed

300 g (10½ oz) rocket (arugula), trimmed and chopped

2 litres (70 fl oz/8 cups) good-quality vegetable stock

125 ml (4 fl oz/½ cup) thin (pouring) cream

crusty bread, to serve

Basil pesto

2 tablespoons pine nuts, toasted (see Tip)

1 garlic clove, crushed

125 g (4½ oz/1 bunch) basil, leaves picked

35 g (1¼ oz/⅓ cup) grated parmesan cheese

60 ml (2 fl oz/¼ cup) olive oil

Place the onion, garlic, beans, rocket and stock in a slow cooker. Gently mix until well combined. Cover and cook on low for 6–8 hours.

Purée the mixture until smooth, using a stick blender, food processor or blender. Stir the cream through. Cover and cook for a further 20 minutes, or until warmed through.

Meanwhile, make the basil pesto. Place the pine nuts, garlic and basil in a food processor and blend until smooth and combined. Add the parmesan and process for a further 1 minute. With the motor running, add the olive oil in a slow steady stream until the pesto is smooth and of a sauce consistency. Season to taste.

Ladle the soup into bowls and sprinkle generously with freshly ground black pepper. Add a healthy dollop of the basil pesto and serve with crusty bread.

TIPS When making the pesto, toasting the pine nuts helps bring out their flavour. Gently cook them in a frying pan over medium–low heat, without any oil, for 3–4 minutes, or until golden brown, keeping a close eye on them and shaking the pan frequently so they don't burn.

This soup can be frozen. Allow the soup to cool, then transfer to an airtight container. Label and date the container and freeze for up to 6 months.

SWEET CORN SOUP HAS ALWAYS BEEN A CHINESE RESTAURANT
FAVOURITE. IT'S THE SLOW ADDITION OF BEATEN EGGS AT THE END OF
THE COOKING PROCESS THAT CREATES ITS DISTINCTIVE SILKY TEXTURE.

Sweet corn soup

SERVES 6 AS A STARTER, 4 AS A MAIN
PREPARATION TIME 15 MINUTES
COOKING TIME 3¼ HOURS

1 tablespoon peanut or vegetable oil

1 brown onion, finely chopped

1 garlic clove, finely chopped

1½ tablespoons finely shredded fresh ginger

4 coriander (cilantro) roots, well rinsed and finely
chopped

1 teaspoon sea salt

80 ml (2½ fl oz/⅓ cup) Chinese rice wine or
dry sherry

4 sweet corn cobs, kernels removed

400 g (14 oz) tin creamed corn

1 litre (35 fl oz/4 cups) good-quality
vegetable stock

2–3 teaspoons light soy sauce

pinch of ground white pepper

2 eggs, lightly beaten

sesame oil, to serve

coriander (cilantro) leaves, to serve

Heat the peanut oil in the insert pan of a slow cooker or a
frying pan over medium–low heat. Add the onion, garlic,
ginger, coriander root and salt and sauté for 7–8 minutes,
without browning. Increase the heat to medium–high, add the
Chinese rice wine and cook for 1–2 minutes, or until the liquid
has reduced by two-thirds.

Return the insert pan, if using, to the slow cooker, or transfer
the vegetable mixture to the slow cooker. Add the corn kernels,
creamed corn, stock and soy sauce. Season with white pepper
and stir to combine. Cover and cook on low for 3 hours.

Remove the lid and quickly pour in the beaten eggs, in a slow
stream, while stirring with a fork, until the egg creates small
ribbons. Season to taste with sea salt and freshly ground black
pepper. Serve garnished with a drizzle of sesame oil and
coriander leaves.

THIS HEARTY SOUP IS A GREAT WAY TO INTRODUCE KIDS TO
VEGETABLES LIKE CELERY, WHICH SOFTENS AND MELLOWS WITH SLOW
COOKING. TO MAKE THIS VEGAN, LEAVE OUT THE PARMESAN AND
TOP WITH TOASTED PEPITAS AND SUNFLOWER SEEDS INSTEAD.

Minestrone

SERVES 4–6
PREPARATION TIME 15 MINUTES
COOKING TIME 5½ HOURS

2 tablespoons olive oil

1 brown onion, finely chopped

2 garlic cloves, crushed

2 celery stalks, thinly sliced

2 carrots, halved lengthways and thinly sliced

small handful basil, leaves picked, stalks finely
chopped

400 g (14 oz) tin diced tomatoes

2 x 400 g (14 oz) tins cannellini or borlotti beans,
drained and rinsed

1.25 litres (44 fl oz/5 cups) good-quality
vegetable stock

100g (3½ oz) spaghetti, broken into
approximately 3 cm (1¼ inch) lengths

2 zucchini (courgettes), quartered lengthways,
thinly sliced

35 g (1¼ oz/⅓ cup) finely grated parmesan
cheese, to serve

Put the oil, onion, garlic, celery, carrot, chopped basil stalks
(not leaves), tomatoes, beans and stock into the slow cooker
and season with sea salt and freshly ground black pepper.
Stir gently, then cook on low for 5 hours.

Add the spaghetti and zucchini and cook for 30 minutes, or
until the pasta and vegetables are tender.

Serve topped with the grated parmesan and basil leaves
scattered over. Do not allow this soup to sit too long after
cooking because the pasta will overcook.

DALS AND CURRIES

Yellow dal with spinach (chana dal)

SERVES 4
PREPARATION TIME 5 MINUTES
COOKING TIME 4¼ HOURS

50 g (1¾ oz) ghee or butter

1 teaspoon ground turmeric

1 teaspoon chilli powder

1 teaspoon cumin seeds

1 red onion, coarsely grated

1 tablespoon finely grated fresh ginger

2 garlic cloves, crushed or finely chopped

2 long green chillies, thinly sliced

200 g (7 oz/1 cup) chana dal, rinsed (see Tip)

75 g (2¾ oz) baby spinach leaves

roti or other Indian flatbread, to serve

Photo shown on page 48.

Heat the ghee in the insert pan of a slow cooker or a frying pan over medium heat. Cook the turmeric, chilli powder, cumin seeds, onion, ginger, garlic and half of the sliced chilli for about 5 minutes until fragrant and soft.

Return the insert pan, if using, to the slow cooker, or transfer the mixture to the slow cooker, then add the chana dal and 1.25 litres (44 fl oz/5 cups) of water. Cook on high for 4 hours or until the dal is tender and has broken down.

Stir in the spinach and cook for 5 minutes, or until wilted. Season well with sea salt.

Serve with the remaining sliced chilli and flatbread.

TIPS If you can't find chana dal, substitute yellow split peas, but keep in mind that they may take longer to cook.

For meat eaters, this dal also makes a lovely side dish with meat or fish curries and freezes particularly well.

THIS RICH AND ROBUST DAL FROM NORTHERN INDIA IS THE PERFECT WARMING VEGETARIAN MEAL. IT'S ALSO GREAT AS PART OF A SELECTION OF INDIAN DISHES. REMEMBER, THE KIDNEY BEANS AND BLACK LENTILS WILL NEED TO SOAK OVERNIGHT BEFORE COOKING.

Dal makhani

SERVES 4
PREPARATION TIME 10 MINUTES (+ OVERNIGHT SOAKING)
COOKING TIME 3½ HOURS

3 tablespoons ghee or butter

1 brown onion, finely chopped

2 tomatoes, coarsely chopped

2 garlic cloves, crushed

1 tablespoon finely grated fresh ginger

1 cinnamon stick

¾ teaspoon chilli powder

1½ teaspoons ground cumin

1 tablespoon tomato paste (concentrated purée)

65 g (2½ oz/⅓ cup) dried red kidney beans, soaked overnight, drained and rinsed

210 g (7½ oz/1 cup) black lentils, soaked overnight, drained and rinsed

80 ml (2½ fl oz/⅓ cup) thin (pouring) cream

Greek-style yoghurt, mint sprigs and roti, to serve

Photo shown on page 48.

Heat the ghee in a large saucepan over medium heat. Cook the onion for 4 minutes until softened. Add the tomato, garlic, ginger, cinnamon, chilli and cumin and cook for a further 2 minutes until fragrant. Add the tomato paste and cook for 1 minute, then add the beans. Pour in 750 ml (26 fl oz/ 3 cups) of water, scraping the base of the pan to deglaze, then bring to a low boil and cook for 15 minutes.

Transfer to the slow cooker and add the lentils. Cook on high for 3 hours, or until the beans and lentils are tender.

Discard the cinnamon stick, then season the dal with sea salt and stir in the cream. Serve with yoghurt, mint sprigs and roti.

DAL MAKHANI

YELLOW DAL
WITH SPINACH

Green curry of tofu and vegetables

SERVES 4
PREPARATION TIME 15 MINUTES
COOKING TIME 2½ HOURS

300 g (10½ oz) orange sweet potato, peeled, cut into 1 cm (½ inch) dice

8 baby corn

3 tablespoons green curry paste, to taste

500 ml (17 fl oz/2 cups) coconut cream

300 g (10½ oz) firm tofu, cut into 3 cm (1¼ inch) chunks

2 zucchini (courgettes), thickly sliced

60 g (2¼ oz) green beans, trimmed and cut into 3 cm (1¼ inch) lengths

250 g (9 oz/1 bunch) broccolini, washed and halved lengthways

1–2 tablespoons soy sauce

2 tablespoons lime juice

6 kaffir lime leaves, finely shredded (see Tip)

steamed jasmine rice, to serve

Optional extras

Thai basil leaves

1 long green chilli, thinly sliced

Place the sweet potato and baby corn in the slow cooker. In a small bowl, whisk the curry paste and coconut cream until smooth, then pour over the vegetables. Cover and cook on high for 2 hours, or until the sweet potato is tender.

Stir in the tofu, zucchini, beans, broccolini and 1 tablespoon of the soy sauce. Cover and cook for a further 30 minutes, or until all the green vegetables have softened.

Stir the lime juice and half the lime leaves through the curry. Check the seasoning, adding the other tablespoon of soy sauce if the curry needs more saltiness.

Stir in the Thai basil leaves, if using. Garnish with the remaining lime leaves, scatter over the green chilli, if using, and serve with steamed rice.

TIP Kaffir lime leaves are available from greengrocers or Asian grocers. They are sometimes just labelled 'lime leaves' and can be frozen for later use.

COCONUT VINEGAR GIVES THIS EXCEPTIONALLY PRETTY AND NUTRITIOUS CURRY ITS DISTINCTIVE FLAVOUR. BUT YOU COULD USE ANY MILD WHITE VINEGAR INSTEAD – JUST ADD HALF THE AMOUNT TO START WITH AND THEN ADJUST TO TASTE.

Beetroot curry

SERVES 4
PREPARATION TIME 10 MINUTES
COOKING TIME 7 HOURS

60 g (2¼ oz) ghee or butter

2 small red onions, halved, thinly sliced

3 garlic cloves, finely chopped

1½ teaspoons cumin seeds

1½ teaspoons brown mustard seeds

2 tablespoons fresh or dried curry leaves

3 long green chillies, thinly sliced

1.5 kg (3 lb 5 oz/2 large bunches) baby beetroot (beets), peeled and quartered, leaves and stems kept separate and cut into 5 cm (2 inch) pieces

100 ml (3½ fl oz) coconut vinegar (see Tip)

400 ml (14 fl oz) tin coconut milk, shaken

steamed rice, to serve

Heat the ghee in the insert pan of a slow cooker or a large frying pan over medium heat and cook the onion, garlic, cumin seeds, mustard seeds, curry leaves and half the chilli for 4 minutes.

Return the insert pan, if using, to the slow cooker, or transfer the mixture to the slow cooker and add all the remaining ingredients except the beetroot stems and leaves. Cook on low for 6½ hours, or until the beetroot is tender.

Stir in the beetroot stems and leaves and cook for a further 30 minutes until wilted.

Check the seasoning, adding sea salt and freshly ground black pepper if needed, then serve with the remaining chilli and steamed rice.

TIP You can find coconut vinegar at Indian grocers and speciality food shops.

Fragrant red lentil dal

SERVES 4–6
PREPARATION TIME 15 MINUTES
COOKING TIME 4 HOURS

305 g (10¾ oz/1½ cups) red lentils or
   325 g (11½ oz/1½ cups) brown lentils

2 tomatoes, finely chopped

2 garlic cloves, crushed

2 teaspoons finely chopped fresh ginger

1 long green chilli, finely chopped

2 tablespoons coriander (cilantro) leaves,
   chopped, plus extra to garnish

2 teaspoons ground turmeric

½ teaspoon ground cinnamon

¼ teaspoon ground cardamom

500 ml (17 fl oz/2 cups) good-quality
   vegetable stock

40 g (1½ oz) ghee

1 brown onion, thinly sliced

1 teaspoon garam masala

½ teaspoon mustard seeds

½ teaspoon cumin seeds

warm naan, to serve

Rinse and drain the lentils. Place in the slow cooker with the tomato, garlic, ginger, chilli, coriander, turmeric, cinnamon and cardamom. Pour in the stock and 500 ml (17 fl oz/2 cups) of water and gently mix together. Cover and cook on low for 4 hours, or until the lentils are soft.

Meanwhile, heat 30 g (1 oz) of the ghee in a frying pan over high heat. Add the onion and cook, stirring, for 8–10 minutes until dark brown. Remove to a plate.

Heat the remaining ghee in the pan until it is almost smoking, then add the garam masala, mustard seeds and cumin seeds. Cook, stirring, for 30 seconds, then add the spices to the lentils and stir them through. Season to taste with sea salt.

Serve the lentils scattered with the fried onion and extra coriander leaves, with naan on the side.

THIS HEARTY, WARMING CURRY HAS A DELICIOUS NUTTY FLAVOUR, THANKS TO THE TOASTED COCONUT. IF ADDITIONAL VEGETABLES ARE DESIRED, ADD STIR-FRIED SPINACH OR A SIMPLE SIDE OF STEAMED PEAS OR SNOW PEAS.

Chickpea and tomato curry with toasted coconut

SERVES 4
PREPARATION TIME 15 MINUTES
COOKING TIME 4¼ HOURS

45 g (1½ oz/½ cup) desiccated coconut

2 tablespoons vegetable oil

1 brown onion, halved and thinly sliced

4 garlic cloves, coarsely chopped

1 tablespoon finely grated fresh ginger

2 teaspoons ground coriander

2 teaspoons ground cumin

1 cinnamon stick or ½ teaspoon ground cinnamon

¼ teaspoon freshly ground black pepper

1 teaspoon ground turmeric

½ bunch coriander (cilantro), leaves and stalks separated

2 x 400 g (14 oz) tins chickpeas, drained and rinsed

2 fresh or dried bay leaves, scrunched

2 teaspoons brown sugar

2 x 400 ml (14 fl oz) tins coconut milk, shaken

4 ripe tomatoes, quartered

steamed rice, naan or roti, to serve

Heat a medium frying pan over medium heat and add the desiccated coconut. Toast, shaking the pan regularly, for 2–3 minutes until lightly golden. Remove from the pan and set aside.

Heat the oil in the same frying pan over medium heat and fry the onion, garlic and ginger for 6–8 minutes until lightly golden.

Add the ground coriander, cumin, cinnamon, black pepper and turmeric and cook for 1 minute, stirring regularly with a wooden spoon and scraping the base of the pan. Transfer the mixture to the slow cooker.

Add 2 tablespoons of water to the frying pan and swirl around to loosen any of the spice mixture left in the pan. Add to the slow cooker with the coriander stalks, chickpeas, bay leaves, sugar and coconut milk and season well with sea salt. Cook on low for 3 hours.

While the curry is cooking, remove the seeds from the tomatoes using a teaspoon. Coarsely chop the tomatoes.

Stir in the tomato and continue to cook for a further 1 hour or until the sauce has thickened.

Stir three-quarters of the toasted coconut into the curry, then serve accompanied by rice, naan or roti with the coriander leaves and remaining coconut scattered over.

THIS ROBUST SOUTH AFRICAN CURRY IS PACKED WITH FLAVOUR,
THE ONIONS AND GARLIC ENHANCED BY THE ADDITION OF
ASAFOETIDA. SERVE IT OVER A BOWL OF STEAMED RICE
FOR A SIMPLE BUT SATISFYING MEAL.

South African red kidney bean curry

SERVES 4
PREPARATION TIME 15 MINUTES (+ OVERNIGHT SOAKING)
COOKING TIME 3½ HOURS

2 tablespoons ghee or butter

1 large brown onion, coarsely chopped

3 garlic cloves, crushed or finely chopped

3 small green chillies, finely chopped

1 tablespoon finely grated fresh ginger

½ teaspoon brown mustard seeds

½ teaspoon asafoetida (see Tip)

½ teaspoon ground coriander

2 teaspoons garam masala

1 dried long red chilli

3 tomatoes, finely chopped

3 tablespoons curry leaves

2 teaspoons tomato paste (concentrated purée)

290 g (10¼ oz/1½ cups) dried red kidney beans,
soaked overnight, drained and rinsed

flatbread, steamed rice, fried curry leaves and
chopped tomato and cucumber, to serve

Heat the ghee in a large saucepan over medium heat and cook the onion for 4 minutes until softened. Add the garlic, green chilli, ginger and dried spices and cook for 2 minutes until fragrant.

Transfer to the slow cooker, along with the tomato, curry leaves and tomato paste. Add the beans to the saucepan, then pour in 500 ml (17 fl oz/2 cups) of water. Bring to the boil and cook for 15 minutes, then transfer to the slow cooker. Cook on high for 3 hours.

Season to taste with sea salt and freshly ground black pepper, then serve with flatbread, rice, fried curry leaves and chopped tomato and cucumber.

TIP Asafoetida is a pungent ingredient commonly used in Indian vegetarian cooking.

MASSAMAN CURRIES AREN'T GENERALLY SPICY BECAUSE THE PASTE THAT MAKES UP THE BASE OF THE CURRY IS MADE OF AROMATICS — SUCH AS CINNAMON, CARDAMOM, CLOVES, STAR ANISE AND CUMIN — RATHER THAN CHILLI. MASSAMAN CURRIES ARE, ON THE WHOLE, FAMILY FRIENDLY.

Brown lentil and vegetable massaman curry

SERVES 4
PREPARATION TIME 10 MINUTES
COOKING TIME 3 HOURS 10 MINUTES

1 small red or brown onion, cut into thin wedges

1 tablespoon finely grated fresh ginger

2 garlic cloves, crushed or finely chopped

1 tablespoon massaman curry paste, or to taste

400 ml (14 fl oz) tin coconut milk, shaken

2 red or yellow capsicums (peppers), seeds and membranes discarded, coarsely chopped

200 g (7 oz) Swiss brown or button mushrooms, quartered

400 g (14 oz) tin brown lentils, drained and rinsed

125 g (4½ oz) snow peas (mangetout), ends trimmed, halved

1 lime, quartered

1 teaspoon sugar

2 teaspoons soy sauce or fish sauce (see Tip)

steamed jasmine rice, to serve

coriander (cilantro) leaves, to serve (optional)

Put the onion, ginger, garlic, curry paste and coconut milk into the slow cooker and stir to combine. Add the capsicum, mushrooms and lentils and cook on low for 3 hours.

Add the snow peas and cook for 5–10 minutes until just tender. Stir in the juice of 1 lime quarter, the sugar and soy sauce. Taste the curry, adding a little more sugar, lime juice or soy sauce to balance the flavours of sweet, sour and salty.

Serve with rice, with the coriander leaves scattered over and the remaining lime wedges for squeezing over.

TIP If you are eating vegetarian for health reasons rather than ethical reasons, you could use fish sauce instead of soy.

Yellow curry with vegetables

SERVES 4
PREPARATION TIME 30 MINUTES
COOKING TIME 3 HOURS

100 g (3½ oz) cauliflower

1 long, thin eggplant (aubergine)

1 small red capsicum (pepper), seeds and membranes discarded

1–2 tablespoons yellow curry paste, to taste

500 ml (17 fl oz/2 cups) coconut cream

125 ml (4 fl oz/½ cup) good-quality vegetable stock

150 g (5½ oz) green beans

2 small zucchini (courgettes)

150 g (5½ oz) baby corn

1½ tablespoons soy sauce

2 teaspoons grated palm sugar (jaggery) or brown sugar

1 small red chilli, seeded and chopped

coriander (cilantro) leaves, to garnish

steamed rice, to serve

Chop the cauliflower into florets. Cut the eggplant and capsicum into 1 cm (½ inch) slices.

Put the cauliflower, eggplant and capsicum in the slow cooker. Add the curry paste, coconut cream and stock. Cover and cook on low for 2 hours, or until the cauliflower is tender.

While the curry is cooking, trim the beans and chop into 3 cm (1¼ inch) lengths and cut the zucchini into 1 cm (½ inch) slices.

Stir in the zucchini, beans, corn, soy sauce and palm sugar and cook for a further 1 hour, or until all the vegetables are tender.

Scatter over the chilli and coriander and serve with steamed rice.

THANKS TO THE BROWN LENTILS, THIS RICHLY FLAVOURED
CURRY IS A GOOD SOURCE OF BOTH PROTEIN AND IRON.

Indian-style vegetable curry

SERVES 4
PREPARATION TIME 15 MINUTES
COOKING TIME 5½ HOURS

1 brown onion, finely chopped

2 teaspoons finely grated fresh ginger

3 tablespoons mild curry paste, such as balti

small handful curry leaves (see Tip)

375 ml (13 fl oz/1½ cups) good-quality
vegetable stock

350 g (12 oz/2¾ cups) cauliflower florets

300 g (10½ oz) sweet potato, peeled and cut
into 2 cm (¾ inch) chunks

2 tomatoes, chopped

3 tablespoons plain yoghurt

400 g (14 oz) tin brown lentils, drained and rinsed

45 g (1½ oz/1 cup) baby spinach leaves

140 g (5 oz/1 cup) frozen peas, thawed

1 zucchini (courgette), sliced

3 tablespoons chopped coriander (cilantro) leaves

steamed basmati rice, to serve

Put the onion, ginger, curry paste, curry leaves and stock in the slow cooker. Add the cauliflower, sweet potato and tomato and gently mix together. Cover and cook on low for 4–5 hours, or until all the vegetables are tender.

Stir in the yoghurt, lentils, spinach, peas, zucchini and half the coriander. Turn the slow cooker setting to high. Cover and cook for a further 30 minutes, or until the spinach has wilted.

Scatter over the remaining coriander and serve with steamed rice.

TIP Curry leaves are highly aromatic and used extensively in Sri Lankan and southern Indian cooking, particularly in curries. They are available in Asian grocers, selected greengrocers and larger supermarkets.

Vietnamese vegetable curry

SERVES 4
PREPARATION TIME 15 MINUTES
COOKING TIME 3½ HOURS

1 tablespoon Thai yellow curry paste

2 teaspoons ground cumin

1 teaspoon ground coriander

1 teaspoon ground turmeric

10 cm (4 inch) piece lemongrass, white part only,
thinly sliced or finely grated

3 garlic cloves, crushed or finely chopped

1 tablespoon vegetable oil

2 Asian shallots (or small onions), thinly sliced

1 small red chilli, finely chopped (optional)

4 kaffir lime leaves, torn

400 ml (14 fl oz) tin coconut milk, shaken

1 teaspoon brown sugar

4 carrots, halved lengthways, cut into 1 cm
(½ inch) slices

230 g (8 oz) baby corn, halved

350–400 g (12–14 oz) or about half a Chinese
cabbage (wong bok), halved lengthways
then thinly sliced

2 teaspoons soy sauce

1 lime, quartered (optional)

steamed rice or noodles, to serve

Put the curry paste, cumin, coriander, turmeric, lemongrass and garlic in a spice grinder or small food processor – or use a pestle and mortar – and grind to a paste.

Heat the oil in the insert pan of a slow cooker or a small frying pan over medium heat and fry the shallots for 2 minutes. Add the paste and fry for 2 minutes or until fragrant.

Return the insert pan, if using, to the slow cooker, or transfer the mixture to the slow cooker with the chilli, lime leaves, coconut milk, sugar, carrot and baby corn. Season with sea salt and cook on low for 3 hours.

Add the Chinese cabbage and cook for a further 30 minutes.

Stir in the soy sauce and squeeze in the juice from 1 lime quarter, if using.

Serve accompanied by rice or noodles, with the remaining lime for squeezing over, if using.

PANEER IS A CHEESE COMMONLY FOUND IN SOUTHEAST ASIAN CUISINE AND PARTICULARLY IN INDIAN DISHES. THE COCONUT MILK IN THIS CURRY IS OPTIONAL – IT IS JUST A LITTLE RICHER WITH IT ADDED.

Indian curry with paneer, cauliflower and peas

SERVES 4
PREPARATION TIME 15 MINUTES
COOKING TIME 3¼ HOURS

2 tablespoons vegetable oil

1 brown onion, halved and thinly sliced

2 garlic cloves, crushed or finely chopped

1 tablespoon finely grated fresh ginger

2 teaspoons garam masala

2 tablespoons mild Indian curry paste, such as rogan josh

1 small cauliflower (400–500 g/14 oz–1 lb 2 oz), cut into small florets

200 g (7 oz) paneer, cubed (see Tip)

165 ml (5¼ fl oz) coconut milk (optional)

200 g (7 oz) frozen peas, thawed

2 tablespoons seed crunch topping (see page 9), toasted pepitas (pumpkin seeds) or cashew nuts, to serve (optional)

basmati rice, to serve

Heat the oil in the insert pan of a slow cooker or a medium frying pan over medium heat and cook the onion, garlic and ginger for 5 minutes. Add the garam masala and curry paste and cook for 2 minutes until fragrant.

Off the heat, add 250 ml (9 fl oz/1 cup) of water to the frying pan or insert pan and stir with a wooden spoon, scraping the base of the pan to get the bits of flavour stuck to the bottom. Return the insert pan to the slow cooker or transfer the mixture to the slow cooker.

Add the cauliflower, season with sea salt and freshly ground black pepper, and cook on low for 2 hours.

Add the paneer and coconut milk, if using, and cook for a further 1 hour.

Stir in the peas and cook for a final 15 minutes while cooking the rice.

Serve over rice and scatter with the seed crunch or your choice of topping.

TIP Paneer is available from the cheese section of many supermarkets, or in Indian and Asian grocers.

THIS BROTH CONTAINS SEVERAL OF MY FAVOURITE FLAVOURS OF ASIAN COOKING BUT WITHOUT THE SPICE – UNLESS YOU WANT IT, IN WHICH CASE IT CAN BE ADDED AT THE END. LEMONGRASS, GINGER AND LIME LEAVES BLEND TOGETHER BEAUTIFULLY AS THEY SLOW COOK IN COCONUT MILK.

Fragrant tofu and vegetables in coconut broth

SERVES 4
PREPARATION TIME 20 MINUTES
COOKING TIME 3 HOURS 5 MINUTES

½ bunch coriander (cilantro), (optional)

10 cm (4 inch) piece lemongrass stalk, white part only, cut in half lengthways and crushed with a wooden spoon or rolling pin

3 kaffir limes leaves, scrunched up

2 garlic cloves, crushed or finely chopped

1 French shallot, finely chopped

5 cm (2 inch) piece fresh ginger, peeled and finely grated

400 g (14 oz) butternut pumpkin (squash), peeled and seeded, cut into 1 cm (½ inch) dice

400 ml (14 fl oz) tin coconut milk, shaken

500 ml (17 fl oz/2 cups) good-quality vegetable stock

2 x 400 g (14 oz) tins chickpeas, drained and rinsed

100 g (3½ oz) green beans, ends trimmed cut into 2 cm (¾ inch) lengths

1 lime

2 tablespoons soy sauce (see Tip)

1 teaspoon white or brown sugar

100 g (3½ oz) snow peas (mangetout), ends trimmed, thinly sliced

200 g (7 oz) tofu puffs, cut in half (see Tip)

200 g (7 oz) egg noodles (optional)

1 long red chilli, thinly sliced (optional)

Pick the leaves from the coriander, if using, and set aside for serving. Finely chop the stems. Put the stems, lemongrass, lime leaves, garlic, shallot, ginger, pumpkin, coconut milk, stock and chickpeas in the slow cooker and cook on low for 3 hours.

When the broth has 15 minutes left to cook, put the beans into a heatproof bowl and cover with boiling water for 10 minutes. (If using noodles, cook them at this point too, according to the packet instructions.) Juice half the lime and cut the remaining half into wedges. Briefly mash the pumpkin into the broth (do not leave the lid off for too long).

Drain the beans well and add to the slow cooker with the soy sauce, lime juice, sugar and snow peas. Cook for a further 5 minutes. Check seasoning, adding a little extra soy sauce or a pinch of sugar, if necessary. Remove the lemongrass and lime leaves, if you can find them, then add the tofu puffs to the broth and stir once to cover and heat through.

Divide the noodles, if using, among deep bowls and ladle over the broth. Scatter over coriander leaves. Serve sliced chilli on the side for those who like it.

TIPS If your family is eating a vegetarian diet for health rather than ethical reasons, you can replace the soy sauce with fish sauce.

Tofu puffs are fried tofu triangles available from the chilled section of Asian grocers.

THIS CURRY IS MORE AROMATIC THAN SPICY. IF YOU PREFER A SPICIER CURRY, FEEL FREE TO ADD ONE LONG GREEN CHILLI, SEEDED AND CHOPPED, AT THE SAME TIME AS THE ONION.

Sri Lankan butternut pumpkin and cauliflower curry

SERVES 4
PREPARATION TIME 20 MINUTES
COOKING TIME 4 HOURS

80 ml (2½ fl oz/⅓ cup) vegetable oil

1 brown onion, halved and thinly sliced

2 garlic cloves, crushed or finely chopped

5 cm (2 inch) piece fresh ginger, peeled and finely grated

300 g (10½ oz) butternut pumpkin (squash), peeled, seeded and cut into 2–3 cm (¾–1¼ inch) chunks

1 small cauliflower, broken into small florets

400 g (14 oz) tin chickpeas, drained and rinsed

400 g (14 oz) tin brown lentils, drained and rinsed

400 ml (14 fl oz) tin coconut milk, shaken

270 ml (9½ fl oz) tin coconut milk, shaken

steamed basmati rice, to serve

Curry spices

2 teaspoons ground coriander

1 teaspoon ground cumin

1 teaspoon fennel seeds

½ teaspoon ground cardamom

2 star anise

1 cinnamon stick

Toppings (optional)

8–10 curry leaves

1 teaspoon black mustard seeds

Heat 2 tablespoons of the oil in the insert pan of a slow cooker or a frying pan over medium–low heat. Add the onion, garlic and ginger and cook for 8–10 minutes, until the onion is golden, stirring occasionally. Add all the curry spices, season well with sea salt and plenty of freshly ground black pepper and cook for 1 minute.

Return the insert pan, if using, to the slow cooker, or transfer the mixture to the slow cooker. Add the butternut pumpkin, cauliflower, chickpeas, lentils and both tins of coconut milk and stir to combine. Cover and cook on low for 3½–4 hours, or until the vegetables are tender.

Just before serving, heat the remaining 2 tablespoons of oil in a small frying pan over medium heat and fry the curry leaves and mustard seeds, if using, until the seeds pop and the leaves crisp and curl up. Serve the curry with rice and the curry leaves and mustard seeds on top.

THIS MILD BUT TASTY CURRY HAS LOTS OF DELICIOUS SAUCE, SO ENSURE YOU SERVE IT WITH PLENTY OF RICE AND MAYBE SOME NAAN FOR MOPPING IT UP. THERE ARE A FEW DIFFERENT SPICES IN THIS DISH, BUT THEY ARE WHAT GIVE THE CURRY ITS AMAZING FLAVOUR.

Mild southern Indian vegetable curry

SERVES 4
PREPARATION TIME 20 MINUTES
COOKING TIME 3 HOURS 10 MINUTES

2 tablespoons vegetable oil

2 brown onions, halved and thinly sliced

4 garlic cloves, crushed or finely chopped

5 cm (2 inch) piece fresh ginger, peeled and finely grated

½ bunch coriander (cilantro)

1 tablespoon ground coriander

¼ teaspoon ground fenugreek (optional)

½ cinnamon stick or ½ teaspoon ground cinnamon

½ teaspoon ground turmeric

1 teaspoon sea salt

¼ teaspoon freshly ground black pepper

1 bunch baby carrots, scrubbed, ends trimmed, left whole or 3 medium carrots, chopped into 1cm (½ inch) slices

600 g (1 lb 5 oz) waxy potatoes, cut into bite-sized pieces

3 tomatoes, coarsely chopped

400 ml (14 fl oz) tin coconut milk, shaken

100 g (3½ oz) raw cashew nuts

150 g (5½ oz) frozen peas, thawed

steamed basmati rice, to serve

naan, to serve (optional)

1 long green chilli, thinly sliced, to serve (optional)

Heat the oil in the insert pan of a slow cooker or in a frying pan over medium heat. Add the onion, garlic and ginger and cook for 10 minutes, or until the vegetables have softened slightly, stirring occasionally.

Meanwhile, coarsely chop the coriander leaves and finely chop the stems, keeping them separate.

Add all the dry spices, salt and pepper to the pan and cook for 1 minute.

Return the insert pan, if using, to the slow cooker, or transfer the vegetable mixture to the slow cooker. Add the carrots, potato, tomato, coriander stalks and coconut milk, then add 300 ml (10½ fl oz) of water to the coconut milk tin, swirl it around and add to the slow cooker. Stir to combine. Cover and cook on high for 3 hours.

While the curry is cooking, put the cashew nuts in a cold small frying pan over medium heat. Toast, tossing regularly for 3–4 minutes or until golden. Cool slightly then coarsely chop.

Once the vegetables are tender add the peas and half the coriander leaves, if you like, and cook for a further 10 minutes.

Serve the curry with the rice, and naan, too, if desired. Scatter over the cashew nuts, remaining coriander and chilli, if using.

THIS CURRY IS JAM-PACKED FULL OF VEGGIES AND THE ADDITION OF COCONUT MILK AT THE END REALLY ENRICHES ITS FLAVOUR.

Chickpea and vegetable curry

SERVES 4–6
PREPARATION TIME 30 MINUTES
COOKING TIME 2 HOURS 10 MINUTES

3 garlic cloves, crushed

1 long red or green chilli, seeded and chopped

2 tablespoons Indian curry paste (see Tip)

1 teaspoon ground cumin

½ teaspoon ground turmeric

400 g (14 oz) tin chopped tomatoes

250 ml (9 fl oz/1 cup) good-quality vegetable stock

1 red onion, cut into thin wedges

1 large carrot, sliced diagonally into 3 cm (1¼ inch) chunks

250 g (9 oz) orange sweet potato, peeled, sliced diagonally into 3 cm (1¼ inch) chunks

250 g (9 oz) cauliflower, cut into florets

250 g (9 oz) broccoli, cut into florets

2 long, thin eggplants (aubergines), about 100 g (3½ oz) in total, cut into 3 cm (1¼ inch) thick slices

400 g (14 oz) tin chickpeas, drained and rinsed

140 g (5 oz/1 cup) frozen peas, thawed

165 ml (5¼ fl oz) tin coconut milk, shaken

coriander (cilantro) leaves, to garnish

steamed rice, to serve

Combine the garlic, chilli, curry paste, cumin, turmeric, tomatoes and stock in the slow cooker. Stir in the onion, carrot, sweet potato, cauliflower, broccoli, eggplant and chickpeas. Cover and cook on high for 2 hours, or until all the vegetables are tender.

Add the peas and stir through the coconut milk. Cover and cook for a further 10 minutes, or until the peas are just cooked.

Scatter over the coriander and serve with steamed rice.

TIP Add a little more curry paste if you prefer a stronger curry flavour.

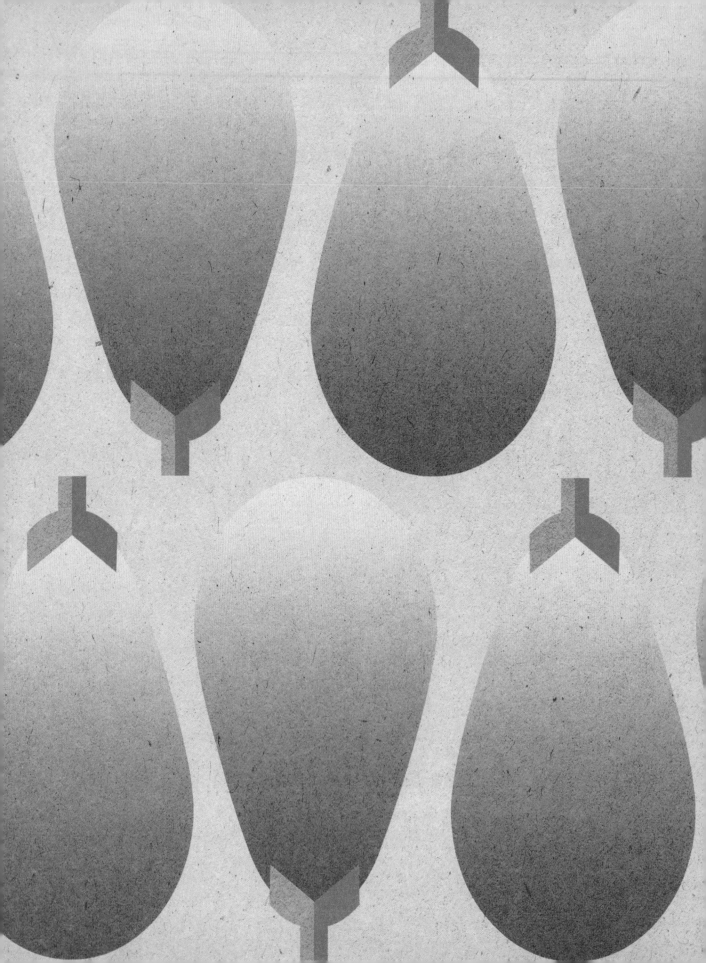

FAMILY FAVOURITES

A LITTLE BIT OF PREPARATION IS NEEDED TO MAKE THIS RICH AND CREAMY MOUSSAKA. HOWEVER, ONCE IT'S IN THE SLOW COOKER YOU CAN LEAVE IT FOR SEVERAL HOURS TO COOK AWAY.

Lentil and mushroom moussaka

SERVES 6
PREPARATION TIME 20 MINUTES
COOKING TIME 4¾ HOURS

160 g (5¾ oz/¾ cup) puy or tiny blue-green lentils

1.2 kg (2 lb 10 oz) eggplants (aubergines), cut into 5 mm (¼ inch) slices

2 tablespoons olive oil, plus extra for brushing

1 onion, finely chopped

2 garlic cloves, crushed or finely chopped

400 g (14 oz) portobello mushrooms, cut into 1 cm (½ inch) dice

2 tablespoons finely chopped oregano

2 tablespoons finely chopped flat-leaf (Italian) parsley

½ teaspoon ground cinnamon

700 ml (24 fl oz) tomato passata (puréed tomatoes)

50 g (1¾ oz) butter

50 g (1¾ oz/⅓ cup) plain (all-purpose) flour

500 ml (17 fl oz/2 cups) milk

1 egg, lightly beaten

100 g (3½ oz) feta cheese, crumbled

flat-leaf (Italian) parsley and rocket (arugula) leaves, to serve

Pick through the lentils to remove any small stones that might still be present. Put the lentils in a saucepan of cold water. Bring to the boil and cook for 10 minutes, then drain.

Meanwhile, preheat a grill (broiler) to high and line a large baking sheet with foil. Lightly brush the eggplant with oil, season well with sea salt and freshly ground black pepper and grill for 5 minutes each side until golden. Set aside.

Heat the oil in a frying pan over medium–high heat. Cook the onion, garlic, mushrooms, oregano, parsley and cinnamon for about 8 minutes until the onion is soft. Stir in the passata and lentils, then season and set aside.

Melt the butter in a saucepan over medium heat. Whisk in the flour and cook for 1 minute, then gradually whisk in the milk. Cook for 4 minutes, stirring constantly, until the sauce thickens. Season to taste, then remove from the heat and whisk in the egg.

Lightly grease the slow cooker. Cover the base with a third of the eggplant slices, then spread over half the lentil mixture. Repeat the layers, finishing with eggplant. Pour over the sauce and scatter with the cheese, then cook on low for 4 hours. If there is still a fair amount of liquid around the edges, remove the lid and leave to cook for a further 20–30 minutes.

Serve with parsley and rocket leaves.

HARISSA IS A NORTH AFRICAN CHILLI PASTE MADE WITH ROASTED CHILLIES AND HERBS AND SPICES SUCH AS CORIANDER SEED AND GARLIC. IT IS COMMONLY ASSOCIATED WITH MOROCCAN COOKING.

Chickpea, apricot and carrot tagine with harissa

SERVES 4
PREPARATION TIME 20 MINUTES
COOKING TIME 3¼–4¼ HOURS

1 tablespoon olive oil

20 g (¾ oz) butter

1 brown onion, thinly sliced

2 garlic cloves, crushed

1 teaspoon ground cumin

½ teaspoon ground ginger

pinch of saffron threads, soaked in 2 teaspoons water

2 x 400 g (14 oz) tins chickpeas, drained and rinsed

1 red capsicum (pepper), seeds and membrane discarded, coarsely chopped

4 carrots, halved lengthways, cut into 2 cm (¾ inch) slices

250 ml (9 fl oz/1 cup) good-quality vegetable stock or water

1 tablespoon harissa paste

200 g (7 oz) dried apricots

35 g (1¼ oz/¼ cup) slivered almonds

200 g (7 oz) baby spinach leaves or 1 bunch English spinach, stalks removed

3 tablespoons coarsely chopped flat-leaf (Italian) parsley

steamed couscous or rice, to serve

green olives, to serve (optional)

100 g (3½ oz) feta cheese, crumbled, to serve (optional)

Heat the oil and butter in the insert pan of a slow cooker or a large frying pan over medium heat and cook the onion and garlic for 5 minutes until the onions are slightly softened. Add the cumin and ginger and cook for 1 minute.

Return the insert pan, if using, to the slow cooker, or transfer the mixture to the slow cooker along with the saffron and its soaking liquid, the chickpeas, capsicum and carrot. Add the stock and harissa paste and season well with sea salt and freshly ground black pepper. Stir to combine, then scatter over the apricots and cook on low for 3–4 hours.

While the tagine is cooking, put the almonds in a cold small frying pan over medium heat. Toast, tossing regularly, for 3–4 minutes or until golden. Set aside.

Add the spinach to the slow cooker and cook for a further 10–15 minutes until wilted.

Serve the tagine over couscous or rice with the almonds and parsley scattered over. Top with olives and feta, if you like.

THE HUMBLE CAULIFLOWER IS HUMBLE NO MORE IN THIS RICH
AND FILLING DISH. CAULIFLOWER FLORETS ARE BURIED IN A TWO-
CHEESE SAUCE WITH ABOUT HALF THE AMOUNT OF PASTA NORMALLY
ASSOCIATED WITH A MAC 'N' CHEESE.

Cauliflower mac 'n' cheese

SERVES 6
PREPARATION TIME 15 MINUTES
COOKING TIME 2–3 HOURS

375 ml (13 fl oz/1½ cups) milk

375 ml (13 fl oz/1½ cups) thin (pouring) cream

3 eggs, lightly beaten

150 g (5½ oz) macaroni

1 cauliflower (about 700–800 g/
  1 lb 9 oz–1 lb 12 oz), broken into largish florets

100 g (3½ oz/1 cup) finely grated parmesan
  cheese

150 g (5½ oz/1½ cups loosely packed) grated
  cheddar cheese

steamed green peas, to serve

Pour the milk and cream into the slow cooker. Gently whisk in the eggs and season with sea salt and freshly ground black pepper. Add the macaroni and stir. Add the cauliflower, parmesan and 100 g (3½ oz/1 cup) of the cheddar and stir to combine, ensuring the macaroni is under the liquid. Sprinkle with the remaining cheddar, then cover and cook on low for 2 hours.

After 2 hours, start checking the pasta. It needs to be cooked until it is al dente. Most of the sauce should be thick but still with some liquid around. At this stage, turn off the cooker and leave for 10–15 minutes. If after 2 hours it still looks very wet, continue to cook, but take care not to overcook the mixture or the sauce will curdle.

Serve with peas on the side.

SERVE THIS AS A SIDE DISH OR A FRESH AND FILLING LUNCH. YOU CAN USE SILVERBEET IN PLACE OF THE RAINBOW CHARD, IF YOU LIKE. REMEMBER THE FETA WILL BE SALTY, SO GO EASY ON THE SALT WHEN SEASONING.

Lentils with chard, dill and feta

SERVES 4
PREPARATION TIME 5 MINUTES
COOKING TIME 3¼ HOURS

400 g (14 oz/2 cups) puy lentils or tiny blue-green lentils, rinsed

1 litre (35 fl oz/4 cups) good-quality vegetable stock

2 garlic cloves, crushed or finely chopped

750 g (1 lb 10 oz) rainbow chard, leaves finely shredded, stems cut into 2 cm (¾ inch) dice

handful coarsely chopped dill

2 spring onions (scallions), thinly sliced

200 g (7 oz) feta cheese, broken into pieces

extra virgin olive oil and lemon wedges, to serve

Put the lentils, stock and garlic into the slow cooker and cook on high for 3 hours, or until the lentils are tender.

Stir in the chard and cook for a further 15 minutes until wilted.

Season with sea salt and freshly ground black pepper, then stir in half of each of the dill, spring onions and feta.

To serve, top with the remaining dill, spring onion, feta and a drizzle of olive oil, with the lemon wedges for squeezing over.

Vegetarian chilli beans

SERVES 4
PREPARATION TIME 15 MINUTES
COOKING TIME 4 HOURS

½ red onion, chopped (use remainder for salsa)

1 red capsicum (pepper), seeds and membranes discarded, chopped

400 g (14 oz) tin chopped tomatoes

1 tablespoon tomato paste (concentrated purée)

2 x 400 g (14 oz) tins red kidney beans, drained and rinsed

3 teaspoons ground coriander

2 teaspoons ground cumin

½ teaspoon chilli powder

2 garlic cloves, crushed

2 dried bay leaves

125 ml (4 fl oz/½ cup) good-quality vegetable stock

85 g (3 oz/⅓ cup) sour cream

2 tablespoons coriander (cilantro) leaves, coarsely chopped (optional)

flour tortillas or steamed rice, to serve (optional)

Avocado salsa

1 avocado, peeled and diced

2 tablespoons lemon juice

1 roma (plum) tomato, seeded and diced

½ red onion, thinly sliced

1–2 tablespoons olive oil

Place the onion, capsicum, tomatoes, tomato paste and beans in the slow cooker. Add the ground coriander, cumin, chilli powder, garlic and bay leaves. Pour in the stock and stir to combine well. Cover and cook on low for 4 hours.

Put all the avocado salsa ingredients in a bowl and gently stir to combine. Season to taste with sea salt and freshly ground black pepper. Cover and refrigerate until required.

Spoon the chilli beans into bowls. Top with a dollop of the sour cream and scatter over the coriander, if using. Serve with the avocado salsa and tortillas or steamed rice, if desired.

YOU CAN FIND DRIED SOYA BEANS AT ASIAN GROCERS AND HEALTH FOOD SHOPS. THIS EASY RECIPE IS A HANDY ONE TO HAVE UP YOUR SLEEVE AS A VEGAN AND GLUTEN-FREE OPTION.

Sweet and sour soya beans

SERVES 4
PREPARATION TIME 5 MINUTES (+ OVERNIGHT SOAKING)
COOKING TIME 6 HOURS

400 g (14 oz/2 cups) dried soya beans, soaked overnight, drained and rinsed

1 carrot, cut into 1 cm (½ inch) dice

125 ml (4 fl oz/½ cup) rice wine vinegar

80 ml (2½ fl oz/⅓ cup) rice syrup (see Tip)

60 ml (2 fl oz/¼ cup) Chinese rice wine

2 tablespoons tamari sauce

1½ tablespoons finely shredded fresh ginger

2 teaspoons sesame oil

chopped cucumber, snow pea (mangetout) shoots, toasted sesame seeds and steamed rice, to serve

Put the soya beans in the slow cooker with 750 ml (26 fl oz/ 3 cups) of water and cook on high for 4 hours.

Stir in the carrot and cook for a further 1 hour.

Drain the soya beans and carrot, then return to the slow cooker. Add the remaining ingredients and cook for 1 hour, or until the beans and carrot are tender.

Serve with cucumber, snow pea shoots, sesame seeds and steamed rice.

TIP Rice syrup is also known as brown rice syrup or rice malt syrup and is an alternative to sugar.

Moroccan ratatouille

SERVES 6
PREPARATION TIME 25 MINUTES
COOKING TIME 4 HOURS 20 MINUTES

80 ml (2½ fl oz/⅓ cup) olive oil, approximately

2 large red onions, cut into 2 cm (¾ inch) chunks

2 eggplants (aubergines), about 450 g (1 lb) each, cut into 2.5 cm (1 inch) chunks

2 large red capsicums (peppers), seeds and membranes discarded, cut into 2.5 cm (1 inch) pieces

2 tablespoons Moroccan spice mix

2 x 400 g (14 oz) tins chopped tomatoes

2 tablespoons tomato paste (concentrated purée)

400 g (14 oz) tin chickpeas, drained and rinsed

750 g (1 lb 10 oz) butternut pumpkin (squash), peeled, seeded and cut into 3 cm (1¼ inch) chunks

2 tablespoons lemon juice

2½ teaspoons honey

110 g (3¾ oz/⅔ cup) pimento-stuffed green olives (optional)

2 tablespoons chopped coriander (cilantro) leaves (optional)

250 g (9 oz/1 cup) Greek-style yoghurt

1 tablespoon chopped mint

steamed couscous or rice, harissa and coriander (cilantro) sprigs, to serve

Heat 1 tablespoon of the olive oil in a large heavy-based frying pan over medium heat. Add the onion and cook, tossing occasionally, for 4 minutes, or until it starts to soften. Transfer to a slow cooker.

Heat another tablespoon of the oil in the pan. Fry the eggplant in two batches for 2 minutes on each side, or until it has softened slightly and is lightly golden, adding a little more oil as necessary. Add to the slow cooker.

Heat another tablespoon of the oil in the pan, then add the capsicum and cook for 3–4 minutes, turning often, until it starts to soften and brown. Stir in the Moroccan spice mix and cook, stirring, for 30 seconds, or until aromatic, then add one tin of the tomatoes, stirring to loosen any stuck-on bits from the base of the pan. Transfer the mixture to the slow cooker.

Add the remaining tomatoes, the tomato paste and the chickpeas to the slow cooker and stir to combine well. Arrange the pumpkin on top. Cover and cook on low for 4 hours, or until the vegetables are very tender but still holding their shape.

Gently stir in the lemon juice, honey, olives and chopped coriander leaves, if using. Season to taste with sea salt and freshly ground black pepper.

Combine the yoghurt and mint. Serve the ratatouille on a bed of steamed couscous or rice, with the minted yoghurt and harissa, and coriander sprigs for those who like it.

CHIPOTLE CHILLIES IN ADOBO SAUCE ADD A FRAGRANT SMOKY
FLAVOUR, RATHER THAN THE TRADITIONAL FIRE OF FRESH CHILLIES.
IF LESS HEAT IS DESIRED, USE FEWER CHILLIES IN THE SAUCE, THEN
SERVE THE REST SEPARATELY FOR THOSE WHO LIKE MORE HEAT.

Three-bean chipotle chilli

SERVES 6
PREPARATION TIME 10 MINUTES
COOKING TIME 5–6 HOURS ON LOW, OR 3–3½ HOURS ON HIGH

2 corn cobs, or 260 g (9¼ oz/1¾ cup) frozen corn kernels, thawed

400 g (14 oz) tin kidney beans

400 g (14 oz) tin cannellini beans

400 g (14 oz) tin black beans

2 garlic cloves, crushed or finely chopped

400 g (14 oz) tin diced or crushed tomatoes

2 teaspoons dried oregano

1 tablespoon Moroccan spice mix

2 tablespoons red wine vinegar

1–2 tablespoons chipotle chillies in adobo sauce, finely chopped (see Tip)

1 large red capsicum (pepper), seeds and membranes discarded, cut into 1 cm (½ in) dice

To serve

low-salt tortilla chips,12–16 large flour tortillas or rice

sour cream, diced avocado, coarsely chopped coriander (cilantro), (optional)

If using fresh corn cobs, lie them on their side on a board and carefully slice off the kernels. If using frozen corn, rinse under hot water in a sieve. Put the corn kernels into the slow cooker.

Drain and rinse all the beans and add to the slow cooker. Add the garlic, tomatoes, oregano, Moroccan spice mix, vinegar, chipotle chilli and adobo sauce and capsicum. Season with sea salt and freshly ground black pepper and stir to combine.

Cook on low for 5–6 hours or on high for 3–3½ hours.

When the chilli is almost cooked, prepare your choice of accompaniment: tortilla chips, large tortillas or rice.

Serve with sour cream, diced avocado and chopped coriander, if using.

TIP Some chipotle chillies in adobo sauce come already chopped up and combined with the sauce. Others are distinct chillies in the sauce; just chop as required, then store the remainder in the fridge.

EGGPLANT IS A DELICIOUS ADDITION TO THIS HEARTY VEGETARIAN CHILLI. IT'S A COMPLETE MEAL ON ITS OWN, BUT IS ALSO DELICIOUS ACCOMPANIED BY YOUR CHOICE OF RICE, CORN CHIPS, AVOCADO AND SOUR CREAM. ADJUST THE AMOUNT OF CHILLI TO SUIT YOUR FAMILY.

Mediterranean vegetable and black bean chilli

SERVES 4–6
PREPARATION TIME 20 MINUTES
COOKING TIME 3¼ HOURS

60 ml (2 fl oz/¼ cup) olive oil

1 red onion, thinly sliced

3 garlic cloves, crushed or finely chopped

2 zucchini (courgettes), coarsely chopped

½ teaspoon mild chilli powder

1 teaspoon ground cumin

½–1 teaspoon smoked paprika

1 red capsicum (pepper), seeds and membranes discarded, coarsely chopped

1 large eggplant (aubergine), coarsely chopped

2 x 400 g (14 oz) tins diced tomatoes

2 x 400 g (14 oz) tins black beans, drained and rinsed

1 teaspoon dried oregano

2 corn cobs or 260 g (9¼ oz/1¾ cups) frozen kernels, thawed

steamed rice, to serve (optional)

To serve (optional)

coarsely chopped coriander (cilantro) leaves

sliced or mashed avocado

sour cream

good-quality corn chips (instead of rice)

Heat 1 tablespoon of oil in a large frying pan over medium–high heat. Fry the onion, garlic and zucchini for 5 minutes. Stir in the chilli powder, cumin and paprika and fry for 1 minute. Transfer to a slow cooker.

Heat the remaining 2 tablespoons of oil in the same frying pan and cook the capsicum and eggplant for 3–4 minutes until softened. Transfer to the slow cooker with the tomatoes, beans and oregano. Season well with sea salt and freshly ground black pepper and cook on low for 3 hours.

If using fresh corn cobs, lie the cobs flat on a board and slice off the kernels. Add fresh or thawed corn to the slow cooker and cook for 10 minutes.

Serve with rice or corn chips and your choice of toppings. Any leftovers can be frozen for later use.

NORTH AFRICAN CHERMOULA PASTE – OFTEN USED WITH MEAT AND FISH – ADDS ZESTY NOTES TO SIMPLY COOKED ROOT VEGETABLES IN THIS TAGINE. SERVE WITH QUINOA OR COUSCOUS FOR A LIGHT BUT WARMING SUPPER.

Chermoula root vegetable tagine

SERVES 4
PREPARATION TIME 10 MINUTES
COOKING TIME 3 HOURS

1 small celeriac, peeled, cut into 4 cm (1½ inch) chunks

1 bunch radishes, any larger ones halved

1 bunch baby beetroot (beets), peeled, any larger ones halved

1 bunch baby carrots, scrubbed, leaving 2 cm (¾ inch) greens on top

Chermoula

60 ml (2 fl oz/¼ cup) extra virgin olive oil

2 garlic cloves, finely chopped

2 teaspoons finely grated fresh ginger

1 large red onion, coarsely grated

½ teaspoon chilli flakes

½ teaspoon ground turmeric

1½ teaspoons ground cumin

4 tablespoons finely chopped flat-leaf (Italian) parsley

4 tablespoons finely chopped coriander (cilantro)

3 tablespoons finely chopped preserved lemon rind

pinch saffron threads, soaked in 1 tablespoon hot water

For the chermoula, place all the ingredients and 80 ml (2½ fl oz/⅓ cup) of water in the slow cooker. Mix well to combine, then season with sea salt and freshly ground black pepper.

Add the celeriac, radishes and beetroot to the slow cooker and toss to coat. Cook on high for 1 hour, then add the carrots and cook for a further 2 hours, or until the vegetables are tender. Check the seasoning and serve.

Black bean and spinach enchiladas

SERVES 4
PREPARATION TIME 25 MINUTES (+ OVERNIGHT SOAKING)
COOKING TIME 2 HOURS 40 MINUTES

220 g (7¾ oz/1 cup) dried black beans, soaked overnight (or 400 g/14 oz tin black beans)

1 tablespoon grapeseed oil or rice bran oil

1 onion, finely chopped

2 garlic cloves, crushed or finely chopped

1 bunch English spinach, washed, coarsely chopped

2 x 400 g (14 oz) tins chopped tomatoes

2 teaspoons ground cumin

1 tablespoon smoked paprika

2 long green chillies, finely chopped

handful coriander (cilantro) roots and stems, washed, finely chopped

1 teaspoon raw sugar

2 teaspoons lime juice

150 g (5½ oz/1½ cups) grated cheddar cheese

12 small corn or flour tortillas

Chunky guacamole

2 ripe avocados, halved

100 g (3½ oz) cherry tomatoes, quartered

handful coriander (cilantro) leaves, chopped

finely grated zest and juice of 1 lime

1 long green chilli, finely chopped

Put the soaked black beans into a large saucepan and cover with water. Bring to the boil, then simmer for 30 minutes until almost tender. (If using a tin of black beans, omit this step.) Drain and rinse the beans – cooked or tinned – then set aside in a bowl.

Meanwhile, heat the oil in a large frying pan over medium heat. Cook the onion and garlic for 5 minutes until the onion is soft. Add the spinach and cook for 2 minutes until wilted. Season with sea salt and freshly ground black pepper and add to the bowl of beans.

Add the tomatoes, cumin, paprika, chilli, coriander roots and stems, sugar and lime juice to the pan. Cook for 2 minutes, stirring, then season. Stir 250 ml (9 fl oz/1 cup) of this tomato sauce and a third of the cheese into the bean mixture, then spoon 4 tablespoons onto each tortilla and roll up to enclose.

Evenly spread 125 ml (4 fl oz/½ cup) of the sauce over the base of the slow cooker. Lay the enchiladas on top, seam-side down, covering each layer with sauce and cheese. Cook on low for 2 hours.

For the guacamole, mash the avocados with a fork. Stir in the remaining ingredients and season to taste.

Serve the enchiladas with the guacamole.

CAPONATA IS A SICILIAN DISH PACKED FULL OF HEALTHY VEGETABLES.
WE'VE TEAMED IT WITH FILLING PUY LENTILS AND A TWIST OF LEMON.

Puy lentils with caponata

SERVES 6
PREPARATION TIME 15 MINUTES
COOKING TIME 6–7 HOURS ON LOW, OR 3–4 HOURS ON HIGH

1 lemon

300 g (10½ oz) puy lentils or tiny blue-green lentils

2 tablespoons olive oil

750 ml (26 fl oz/3 cups) good-quality vegetable stock

1 red onion, cut into thin wedges

3 celery stalks, coarsely chopped

1 red capsicum (pepper), seeds and membranes discarded, coarsely chopped

1 medium eggplant (aubergine), coarsely chopped into 2 cm (¾ inch) chunks

400 g (14 oz) tin diced tomatoes

1 teaspoon sugar

2 tablespoons white wine vinegar

2 garlic cloves, crushed or finely chopped

45 g (1½ oz/¼ cup) capers, rinsed, drained and coarsely chopped

To serve

50 g (1¾ oz/¼ cup) pine nuts

small handful basil leaves

40 g (1½ oz ¼ cup) pitted Kalamata olives, coarsely chopped (optional)

Using a vegetable peeler, peel a wide strip of zest from the lemon. Reserve remaining lemon.

Pick through the lentils to remove any small stones that might still be present. Rinse under running water until the water runs clear.

Put the lentils and lemon peel in a slow cooker with the remaining ingredients, season with freshly ground black pepper, but don't add salt at this stage as it may toughen the lentils, and cook for 6–7 hours on low or 3–4 hours on high.

While the lentils are cooking, put the pine nuts in a cold, small frying pan over medium heat. Toast, tossing regularly for 3–4 minutes until golden. Set aside. Cut the lemon into wedges.

Season the lentils and caponata with sea salt and serve with the pine nuts, basil leaves and olives, if using, scattered over, accompanied by lemon wedges for squeezing over.

IF YOU CAN FIND THEM, PORTOBELLO MUSHROOMS ARE IDEAL FOR THIS DISH, ADDING A GREAT TEXTURE. HOWEVER, SWISS BROWNS OR EVEN THE HUMBLE BUTTON MUSHROOM WILL WORK JUST FINE. THIS STEW IS DELICIOUS SERVED OVER EGG NOODLES OR MASH.

Chickpea, mushroom, carrot and red wine stew

SERVES 4
PREPARATION TIME 15 MINUTES
COOKING TIME 4 HOURS

1 tablespoon olive oil

1 red or brown onion, halved, thinly sliced

2 garlic cloves, crushed or finely chopped

2 carrots, halved lengthways, sliced into 1 cm (½ inch) rounds

500 g (1 lb 2 oz) portobello, Swiss brown or button mushrooms, thickly sliced

2 x 400 g (14 oz) tins chickpeas, drained and rinsed

1 thyme sprig

125 ml (4 fl oz/½ cup) red wine

1 tablespoon tomato paste (concentrated purée)

400 g (14 oz) tin crushed tomatoes

125 ml (4 fl oz/½ cup) thin (pouring) cream

To serve

egg tagliatelle, fettuccine or mashed potato

finely snipped chives

seed crunch topping (see page 9), (optional)

Put all the ingredients except the cream into the slow cooker, season with sea salt and freshly ground black pepper and cook on high for 4 hours, or until the mushrooms are very tender.

Cook your choice of accompaniment 10–20 minutes before the sauce is ready.

If, when you give the stew a good stir, there is a little too much liquid, use a fork to mash a few of the chickpeas into the sauce to help thicken the stew (this may not be necessary).

Stir in the cream, season to taste, then serve the stew over the pasta or mash with the chives scattered over and the seed crunch, if using.

FEEL FREE TO ADJUST THE AMOUNT OF CHILLI, DEPENDING ON YOUR HEAT TOLERANCE. CUBES OF FIRM TOFU OR GREEN BEANS CAN BE USED IN PLACE OF THE SOYA BEANS.

Sichuan chilli eggplant and soya beans

SERVES 4

PREPARATION TIME 10 MINUTES (+ 1 HOUR STANDING)

COOKING TIME 2¾ HOURS

1.25 kg (2 lb 12 oz) eggplants (aubergine), quartered lengthways then cut into 3 cm (1¼ inch) slices

2 teaspoons Sichuan peppercorns

1½ tablespoons sesame oil

4 garlic cloves, crushed or finely chopped

2 teaspoons finely grated fresh ginger

80 ml (2½ fl oz/⅓ cup) Chinese rice wine

80 ml (2½ fl oz/⅓ cup) vegetarian oyster sauce

1 teaspoon chilli flakes

60 ml (2 fl oz/¼ cup) light soy sauce

1½ tablespoons malt vinegar

1 tablespoon coconut sugar or raw sugar

1 tablespoon cornflour (cornstarch)

4 spring onions (scallions), thinly sliced, white and pale parts kept separate from green parts

220 g (7¾ oz/1½ cups) frozen shelled soya beans (edamame), thawed (see Tip)

roasted peanuts, sliced long red chilli, chopped coriander (cilantro) and steamed rice, to serve

Sprinkle the eggplant with salt and set aside in a large colander set over a bowl for 1 hour.

Rinse the eggplant and pat dry with paper towel.

Meanwhile, put the Sichuan peppercorns in a cold, small frying pan over medium heat. Toast, stirring so they don't burn, for 3–4 minutes until fragrant. Coarsely crush.

Working in batches, heat 2 teaspoons of the oil in a large frying pan or wok over medium–high heat and sear a third of the eggplant for 2 minutes each side, then transfer to the slow cooker. Repeat with the remaining oil and eggplant.

In a bowl, combine the peppercorns, garlic, ginger, rice wine, oyster sauce, chilli flakes, soy sauce, vinegar, sugar, cornflour, the white and pale parts of the spring onions and 250 ml (9 fl oz/1 cup) of water. Whisk well, then transfer to the slow cooker. Cook on high for 2¼ hours.

Stir in the soya beans and cook for a further 15 minutes.

Scatter with the spring onion greens, peanuts, chilli and coriander, then serve with rice.

TIP Frozen edamame beans – young soya beans – can be bought from Asian grocers and the freezer section of some supermarkets.

THIS ISN'T JUST A ONE-PAN SLOW COOKER RECIPE. INSTEAD, THE
TOFU IS PAN-FRIED IN A SEASONED COATING, THEN SERVED TOPPED
WITH THE DELICIOUS CACCIATORE SAUCE. YOU CAN LEAVE OUT THE
TOFU AND SERVE THE SAUCE OVER PASTA OR RICE INSTEAD.

Chickpea cacciatore with pan-fried tofu and olives

SERVES 4
PREPARATION TIME 20 MINUTES
COOKING TIME 5½ HOURS

2 tablespoons olive oil

1 large eggplant (aubergine), cut into 1–2 cm
(½–¾ inch) dice

1 brown onion, coarsely chopped

2 garlic cloves, crushed or finely chopped

3 celery stalks, thinly sliced

2 carrots, quartered lengthways, cut into 1 cm
(½ inch) slices

2 x 400 g (14 oz) tins chickpeas, drained
and rinsed

250 ml (9 fl oz/1 cup) dry white wine or extra stock

250 ml (9 fl oz/1 cup) good-quality vegetable stock

400 g (14 oz) tin diced tomatoes

2 tablespoons tomato paste (concentrated purée)

1 fresh or dried bay leaf

2 rosemary sprigs

2 tablespoons white wine vinegar

80 g (2¾ oz/½ cup) pitted Kalamata olives,
halved

2 tablespoons chopped flat-leaf (Italian) parsley

Tofu

300–600 g (10½–1 lb 5 oz) firm tofu

2 tablespoons plain (all-purpose) flour

1 teaspoon dried oregano

2 tablespoons olive oil

Heat the oil in the insert pan of a slow cooker or a large frying
pan over medium–high heat and cook the eggplant for
4–5 minutes until softened. Return the insert pan, if using, to
the slow cooker, or transfer the eggplant to the slow cooker
with the remaining ingredients, except the white wine vinegar,
olives and parsley. Season well with sea salt and freshly ground
black pepper and cook on low for 5 hours.

Stir in the vinegar and olives and cook for a further 30 minutes,
while you make the tofu.

For the tofu, pat each block dry with paper towel then place
between two sheets of paper towel. Put on a plate, put a small
plate on top and weigh down with two food tins or other heavy
weight, to release excess moisture from the tofu. Leave for
20 minutes. (You can omit the pressing stage but the tofu
generally tastes better when it has been pressed.)

Cut each block of tofu into 4 'slabs'. Put the flour in a shallow
dish with the oregano and season with sea salt and freshly
ground black pepper. Dust each tofu slab in the flour. Heat
the oil in a large frying pan over medium–high heat and cook
the tofu, in batches if necessary, for 2–3 minutes on each side
until golden.

Serve the tofu immediately. Put a piece of tofu on each plate
and top with the cacciatore sauce – removing the bay leaf and
rosemary sprigs – and scatter over the parsley.

TOTAL COMFORT FOOD – THAT'S THE ONLY WAY TO DESCRIBE THIS DISH, WHICH IS FILLING, WARMING, NUTRITIOUS AND DELICIOUS. BROWN LENTILS REPLACE THE MORE TRADITIONAL BEEF, MAKING THIS A WELL-BALANCED FAMILY MEAL EVERYONE WILL LOVE.

Lentil and vegetable 'cottage pie'

SERVES 4
PREPARATION TIME 25 MINUTES
COOKING TIME 3¼ HOURS

1 kg (2 lb 4 oz) mashing potatoes, peeled and coarsely chopped

30 g (1 oz) butter

2 tablespoons milk

2 tablespoons olive oil

1 onion, finely chopped

2 garlic cloves, crushed or finely chopped

2 carrots, finely grated

2 zucchini (courgettes), finely grated

1 thyme sprig, leaves stripped

2 teaspoons dried oregano

2 x 400 g (14 oz) tins brown lentils, drained and rinsed

400 g (14 oz) tin diced or crushed tomatoes

2 tablespoons tomato paste (concentrated purée)

peas or your favourite green vegetable, to serve (optional)

Put the potato in a large saucepan of salted water and bring to the boil. Cook for 12–15 minutes until tender. Drain well and return to the pan over low heat to evaporate off any excess liquid. Mash with the butter and milk until smooth. Season with sea salt and freshly ground black pepper.

While the potatoes are cooking, put the remaining ingredients into the slow cooker, season well with sea salt and freshly ground black pepper and mix thoroughly. Turn the slow cooker to low. Spread the mashed potato evenly on top of the vegetables and cook for 3 hours.

Serve, accompanied by peas or other green vegetable.

TIP You will need an extra saucepan for this dish to cook the mashed potato beforehand.

RICE, PASTA AND GRAINS

Butter miso mushroom risotto

SERVES 4
PREPARATION TIME 5 MINUTES
COOKING TIME 1 HOUR 50 MINUTES

1 tablespoon sesame oil

300 g (10½ oz) sushi rice, rinsed

2 garlic cloves, crushed or finely chopped

2 spring onions (scallions), thinly sliced, white and green parts kept separate

4 tablespoons white miso paste

50 g (1¾ oz) butter

400 g (14 oz) mixed Asian mushrooms, such as shiitake (stems discarded and caps sliced), shimeji and enoki

50 g (1¾ oz) baby spinach leaves

toasted sesame seeds, to serve

Heat the oil in a large frying pan over medium heat. Add the rice, garlic and the white parts of the spring onions and stir for 1 minute until the rice grains are well coated. Transfer to the slow cooker.

Whisk the miso paste with 750 ml (26 fl oz/3 cups) of boiling water until dissolved, then pour into the slow cooker. Cook on high for 1¼ hours, stirring halfway through.

Melt 20 g (¾ oz) of the butter in the frying pan over medium–high heat. Add the mushrooms and cook for 3 minutes until slightly softened. Tip the mushrooms into the slow cooker, along with 185 ml (6 fl oz/¾ cup) of boiling water. Stir well, then cook for 15 minutes.

Stir in the remaining butter and the spinach leaves, plus another 185 ml (6 fl oz/¾ cup) of boiling water if needed, and cook for 10–15 minutes until the spinach wilts and the rice is al dente. Check the seasoning.

Scatter with the green parts of the spring onions and the toasted sesame seeds to serve.

THIS IS BIT OF A PLAY ON THE MORE WELL-KNOWN BAKED RICOTTA, BUT WITH ADDED PROTEIN FROM THE QUINOA AND VITAMINS FROM THE KALE. ALL THAT'S NEEDED TO COMPLETE YOUR MEAL IS A REFRESHING CUCUMBER AND MINT SALAD.

Quinoa, kale and ricotta cake

SERVES 6
PREPARATION TIME 10 MINUTES
COOKING TIME 4¼ HOURS

200 g (7 oz/1 cup) tri-colour (red, black and white) quinoa or red quinoa, rinsed thoroughly

150 g (5½ oz/4 cups) finely shredded kale leaves

2 tablespoons extra virgin olive oil, plus extra for greasing

2 spring onions (scallions), thinly sliced

4 garlic cloves, finely chopped

600 g (1 lb 5 oz) ricotta cheese

4 eggs

80 g (2¾ oz/¾ cup) finely grated parmesan cheese

large handful coarsely chopped flat-leaf (Italian) parsley

handful coarsely chopped mint

cucumber chunks and mint sprigs, dressed with olive oil and lemon juice, to serve

Grease the slow cooker with oil and line with baking paper. Lay a clean tea towel (dish towel) on the bench and place the lid of the slow cooker onto the towel. Pull the towel up over the lid, securing the corners around the knob with string or an elastic band – this is to catch condensation, preventing it from dripping onto the cake as it cooks.

Put the quinoa into a saucepan and cover with 1 litre (35 fl oz/ 4 cups) of water. Bring to the boil, then cover with a lid and reduce the heat to low. Cook for 10 minutes, then add the kale and cook for another 2 minutes. Drain the quinoa and kale, then refresh under cold running water. Drain well.

Combine the remaining ingredients in a large bowl and season well with sea salt and freshly ground black pepper. Add the quinoa and kale and mix thoroughly, then spoon into the slow cooker, smoothing the surface of the cake. Put the lid on and cook on low for 4 hours until set and cooked through (see Tip).

Serve with cucumber and mint salad.

TIP A 5.5 litre (192 fl oz/22 cup) slow cooker was used for this recipe. Remember that cooking times may vary depending on the capacity of your cooker, so if yours is bigger or smaller than this, keep an eye on things for the last hour or so of cooking.

ALTHOUGH A STROGANOFF IS TRADITIONALLY MADE WITH MEAT, THIS HEARTY VEGETARIAN VERSION IS PERHAPS EVEN MORE DELICIOUS. IF POSSIBLE, INCORPORATE SOME FLAVOURSOME MUSHROOMS, SUCH AS PORTOBELLO, INTO THE MIX.

Mixed mushroom stroganoff

SERVES 4
PREPARATION TIME 10 MINUTES
COOKING TIME 3 HOURS 10 MINUTES

600 g (1 lb 5 oz) mixed mushrooms, such as Swiss brown, portobello or flat

2 tablespoons olive oil

20 g (¾ oz) butter

2 shallots or 1 small brown onion, finely chopped

2 garlic cloves, crushed or finely chopped

2 teaspoons sweet paprika

2 tablespoons plain (all-purpose) flour

250 ml (9 fl oz/1 cup) good-quality vegetable stock

2 tablespoons tomato paste (concentrated purée)

250 ml (9 fl oz/1 cup) crème fraîche or sour cream

pasta (wide noodles are great), steamed rice or mashed potato, to serve

2 tablespoons coarsely chopped flat-leaf (Italian) parsley

Cut any smaller mushrooms into halves or quarters and cut any larger ones into bite-sized pieces.

Heat the oil and butter in the insert pan of a slow cooker or a large frying pan over medium heat. Cook the shallots, garlic and paprika for 2 minutes. Add the mushrooms and cook for 3–4 minutes until starting to soften. Add the flour and cook for 2 minutes.

Return the insert pan, if using, to the slow cooker, or transfer the mixture to the slow cooker with the vegetable stock, tomato paste and crème fraîche. Season with sea salt and freshly ground black pepper, stir well to combine, then cook on low for 3 hours.

Spoon the mushroom stroganoff over your choice of pasta, rice or mashed potato and scatter over the parsley.

SOFT, GOOEY MACARONI CHEESE MADE WITH BOTH PARMESAN
AND CHEDDAR CHEESES – DELICIOUS!

Two-cheese macaroni

SERVES 4–6
PREPARATION TIME 25 MINUTES (+ 10 MINUTES SOAKING)
COOKING TIME 2–3 HOURS

300 g (10½ oz/2 cups) macaroni

cooking oil spray, olive oil or softened butter,
for brushing

375 ml (13 fl oz/1½ cups) milk

375 ml (13 fl oz/1½ cups) evaporated milk

3 eggs, lightly beaten

½ teaspoon freshly grated nutmeg

3 spring onions (scallions), chopped

125 g (4½ oz) tin corn kernels, drained

100 g (3½ oz/1 cup) finely grated parmesan
cheese

150 g (5½ oz/1½ cups loosely packed) grated
cheddar cheese

snipped chives, to garnish

green salad, to serve

Put the macaroni in a large heatproof bowl. Cover with boiling water and set aside to soften for 10 minutes, stirring occasionally. Drain.

Meanwhile, spray the bowl of the slow cooker with cooking oil spray, or grease well with olive oil or softened butter. Pour the milk and evaporated milk into the slow cooker. Gently whisk in the eggs and nutmeg and season with sea salt and freshly ground black pepper. Stir in the drained macaroni, spring onion, corn, parmesan and 100 g (3½ oz/1 cup) of the cheddar. Scatter over the remaining cheddar. Cover and cook on low for 2 hours.

After 2 hours, start checking the dish. The sauce needs to be thick and still a little wet in the centre and the macaroni needs to be just soft. It may take a further 1 hour to reach this point, but take care not to overcook the mixture or the sauce will curdle.

Sprinkle with chives and serve with a green salad.

TIP Cook this recipe on low heat only.

Three-cheese and silverbeet lasagne

SERVES 4–6
PREPARATION TIME 20 MINUTES
COOKING TIME 3¼ HOURS

80 ml (2½ fl oz/⅓ cup) extra virgin olive oil

750 g (1 lb 10 oz) silverbeet (Swiss chard), leaves finely shredded, stems finely chopped, kept separate

1 small red onion, finely chopped

3 garlic cloves, crushed or finely chopped

large handful basil, stems finely chopped, leaves coarsely chopped

2 tablespoons tomato paste (concentrated purée)

3 x 400 g (14 oz) tins chopped tomatoes

400 g (14 oz) ricotta cheese

100 g (3½ oz/1 cup) finely grated parmesan cheese, plus extra to serve

150 g (5½ oz) bocconcini or mozzarella cheese, cut into small cubes

1 egg, lightly beaten

250–300 g (9–10½ oz) lasagne sheets

green salad, to serve (optional)

Heat 2 tablespoons of the oil in a large frying pan over medium–high heat. Cook the silverbeet stems and onion for 2 minutes, then add the silverbeet leaves and cook for a further 3 minutes until wilted. Drain, squeezing out any excess liquid. Transfer to a large bowl and allow to cool while making the tomato sauce.

Heat the remaining oil in the frying pan over medium–low heat. Add the garlic and basil stems and cook for 3 minutes until golden. Stir in the tomato paste and cook for 1 minute before adding the chopped tomatoes. Season with sea salt and freshly ground black pepper, then simmer for 10 minutes or until the sauce thickens slightly.

Add the three cheeses, egg and basil leaves to the bowl with the silverbeet and mix well. Season with sea salt and freshly ground black pepper.

Transfer about one-third of the tomato sauce to the slow cooker and spread over the base. Arrange a layer of lasagne sheets (about one-third of the sheets) on top of the sauce, snapping to fit if necessary. Top with half of the silverbeet mixture, another layer of lasagne sheets and another third of the sauce. Top with the remaining filling, lasagne sheets and tomato sauce. Cook on low for 3 hours, or until the pasta is tender.

Serve with extra grated parmesan and a green salad, if you like.

FONTINA IS A CHEESE MADE FROM COW'S MILK WITH A MILD NUTTY
FLAVOUR. MANY SUPERMARKETS STOCK IT, BUT IF YOU CAN'T FIND IT,
SUBSTITUTE IT WITH A SWISS CHEESE OR SOME GRATED MOZZARELLA.

Fontina and rosemary risotto

SERVES 4–6
PREPARATION TIME 15 MINUTES
COOKING TIME 1 HOUR

2 tablespoons olive oil

1 brown onion, finely diced

3 garlic cloves, finely chopped

2 tablespoons rosemary leaves, coarsely chopped

440 g (15½ oz/2 cups) arborio rice (see Tip)

200 ml (7 fl oz) white wine

1.4 litres (49 fl oz) good-quality vegetable stock, heated

120 g (4¼ oz/1 cup) roughly grated fontina cheese

50 g (1¾ oz/½ cup) finely grated parmesan cheese, plus extra to serve

40 g (1½ oz) butter, chopped

Heat the olive oil in the insert pan of a slow cooker or a frying pan over medium–low heat. Add the onion and garlic and cook, stirring, for 4–6 minutes until softened. Add the rosemary and rice and stir for 1–2 minutes until the rice is hot. Pour in the wine and stir for 2–3 minutes until it has slightly reduced. Stir in the hot stock and bring to a simmer.

Return the insert pan, if using, to the slow cooker, or transfer the rice mixture to the slow cooker. Cover and cook on high, stirring occasionally, for 35–45 minutes, or until the rice is tender.

Stir the fontina cheese, parmesan and butter through the risotto until it is creamy and combined. Season to taste with sea salt and freshly ground black pepper and serve sprinkled with extra parmesan.

TIP Arborio rice is a short-grain rice perfect for making risotto. You can find arborio in the rice section at the supermarket.

Cheesy zucchini, cherry tomato and pesto pasta bake

SERVES 6
PREPARATION TIME 10 MINUTES
COOKING TIME 2 HOURS 40 MINUTES

2 tablespoons olive oil

2 large zucchini (courgettes), cut into approximately 1 cm (½ inch) dice

250 g (9 oz) cherry tomatoes

125 ml (4 fl oz/½ cup) basil pesto, purchased or see page 39

200 g (7 oz/1½ cups) grated mozzarella cheese

50 g (1¾ oz/½ cup) grated parmesan cheese

500 g (1 lb 2 oz) penne pasta (or your favourite pasta shape)

1.4 litres (49 fl oz) tomato passata (puréed tomatoes)

Heat the oil in the insert pan of the slow cooker or a frying pan over medium heat and cook the zucchini for 5–6 minutes until lightly golden.

Return the insert pan, if using, to the slow cooker, or transfer the zucchini to the slow cooker with the cherry tomatoes, pesto, mozzarella and half the parmesan.

Add the pasta and the passata, then add 185 ml (6 fl oz/¾ cup) of water to the passata container and swirl around. Add the 'tomato water' to the slow cooker, season with sea salt and freshly ground black pepper and stir to combine. Cook on low for 2–2½ hours until the pasta is tender.

Serve with the remaining parmesan scattered over.

JUST BECAUSE YOU'RE VEGETARIAN, THERE'S NO NEED TO MISS OUT ON BOLOGNESE. SLOW COOK LENTILS AND CAULIFLOWER IN A TOMATO SAUCE AND NO-ONE WILL KNOW THE DIFFERENCE!

Cauliflower and lentil 'bolognese'

SERVES 4
PREPARATION TIME 20 MINUTES
COOKING TIME 3-4 HOURS

2 tablespoons olive oil

1 brown onion, finely chopped

2 garlic cloves, crushed or finely chopped

1 small cauliflower, coarsely grated or finely chopped

60 ml (2 fl oz/¼ cup) red or white wine (optional)

2 zucchini (courgettes), finely grated

2 carrots, finely grated

2 celery stalks, finely chopped

400 g (14 oz) tin brown lentils, drained and rinsed

400 g (14 oz) tin diced or crushed tomatoes

100 g (3½ oz/⅓ cup) tomato paste (concentrated purée)

2 teaspoons dried oregano

1 fresh or dried bay leaf (optional)

To serve

spaghetti

finely grated parmesan cheese

small handful fresh basil leaves

green salad

Put all the ingredients into the slow cooker. Season well with sea salt and freshly ground black pepper, stir to combine and cook on low for 3–4 hours, or until the cauliflower is very soft.

Cook the spaghetti according to the packet instructions. Drain, reserving 1–2 tablespoons of the cooking water. Stir the water into the pasta sauce and serve the sauce over the spaghetti.

Scatter over the parmesan and basil leaves, and serve with a green salad.

ALTHOUGH RISOTTO IS TRADITIONALLY MADE WITH RICE, THIS RECIPE USES BARLEY, WHICH IS A GREAT SLOW COOKER SUBSTITUTE. ADDING BEETROOT TO THE RISOTTO GIVES IT A WONDERFUL PINK COLOUR.

Barley and beetroot risotto with goat's cheese and tarragon

SERVES 4
PREPARATION TIME 15 MINUTES (+ SOAKING)
COOKING TIME 4 HOURS

2 tablespoons olive oil

40 g (1½ oz) butter

1 leek, white part only, washed, thinly sliced

2 garlic cloves, crushed or finely chopped

3 tarragon stalks

1–2 large beetroot (beets) (about 400 g/14 oz), peeled and diced

1.25 litres (44 fl oz/5 cups) good-quality vegetable stock

300 g (10½ oz/1½ cups) barley (soaked, drained and rinsed, see Tip)

100 g (3½ oz) goat's cheese

Heat the oil and half the butter in the insert pan of a slow cooker or a medium frying pan over medium heat and cook the leek and garlic for 5 minutes or until softened. Season with sea salt and freshly ground black pepper.

Meanwhile, pick the tarragon leaves, reserving them for serving. Finely chop the stems. Return the insert pan, if using, to the slow cooker, or transfer the mixture to the slow cooker along with the diced beetroot and the chopped tarragon stems and cook on low for 1 hour.

Add the stock to the slow cooker with the barley, season with sea salt and freshly ground black pepper and stir to combine. Cover and cook on high for 3 hours, or until the barley and beetroot are tender.

Stir the risotto and add a little extra hot stock or water if the risotto is too thick.

Coarsely chop the tarragon leaves and stir half into the risotto with the remaining butter and half the goat's cheese. Serve the risotto with the remaining goat's cheese dolloped on top and the remaining tarragon leaves scattered over. Alternatively, serve all the goat's cheese at the table for those who like it.

TIP To aid digestion, it's advisable to soak the barley in cold water at room temperature for about 6 hours or overnight before using. If you have any, add 2 teaspoons plain yoghurt to help with a little fermentation.

IF YOU ARE USING A SLOW COOKER THAT HAS A CAPACITY GREATER THAN 4.5 LITRES (157 FL OZ/18 CUPS), YOU MAY WANT TO INCREASE THE TOMATO PASTA SAUCE BY HALF AGAIN, OR IF YOUR COOKER IS PARTICULARLY LARGE, DOUBLE IT. OTHERWISE, THE CANNELLONI MAY BE TOO DRY.

Zucchini and ricotta cannelloni

SERVES 4–6
PREPARATION TIME 20 MINUTES
COOKING TIME 3 HOURS

2 zucchini (courgettes), grated

500 g (1 lb 2 oz) ricotta cheese

2 teaspoons chopped rosemary

250 g (9 oz) dried cannelloni (about 20 tubes)

700 g (1 lb 9 oz) tomato pasta sauce

190 g (6¾ oz/1½ cups loosely packed) grated mozzarella cheese

large handful basil, chopped

green salad, to serve

Place the zucchini, ricotta and rosemary in a bowl. Season with sea salt and freshly ground black pepper and mix together well.

Using a teaspoon (see Tip), fill the cannelloni tubes with the ricotta mixture.

Grease the base of your slow cooker and place half the cannelloni in it. Cover with half the tomato pasta sauce, then sprinkle with half the cheese and half the basil. Top with another layer of cannelloni, then the remaining pasta sauce, cheese and basil. Cover and cook on high for 3 hours, or until the pasta is al dente and the cheese has melted.

Serve with a green salad.

TIP You might find it easier to spoon the mixture into a disposable zip-lock bag, then snip off the corner and fill the cannelloni tubes that way.

TRADITIONALLY RISOTTO IS MADE ON THE STOVETOP AND STIRRED FREQUENTLY, BUT A GREAT RESULT CAN BE ACHIEVED IN A SLOW COOKER WITHOUT ALL THE STIRRING. SERVE IT WITH THE PANGRATTATO TOPPING FOR EXTRA CRUNCH AND FLAVOUR.

Red capsicum and pea risotto

SERVES 4–6
PREPARATION TIME 10 MINUTES
COOKING TIME 1½ HOURS

1.6 litre (55½ fl oz) good-quality vegetable stock

1 tablespoon olive oil

2 red capsicums (peppers), seeds and membranes discarded, cut into 1 cm (½ inch) dice

1 red or brown onion, finely chopped

2 garlic cloves, crushed or finely chopped

1 thyme sprig

440 g (15½ oz/2 cups) arborio rice

210 g (7½ oz/1½ cups) frozen peas, thawed

20 g (¾ oz) butter

pangrattato topping (see page 8) (optional)

25 g (1 oz/¼ cup) finely grated parmesan cheese, to serve (optional)

Bring the stock to the boil in a saucepan, then remove from the heat.

Meanwhile, put the oil, capsicum, onion, garlic, thyme and rice into the slow cooker. Add the hot stock and stir to combine. Cook for 1 hour and 20 minutes on low.

Stir in the peas and cook for a further 10–15 minutes until the rice is cooked al dente. It should still feel a tiny bit firm to the bite. Stir in the butter.

Serve topped with the pangrattato, if you like, and the parmesan.

SLOWLY COOKING THE TOMATOES AND CAPSICUM CREATES A RICH, SWEET SAUCE THAT IS PERFECT FOR SPOONING OVER PASTA. LENTILS ADD EXTRA PROTEIN. MAKE DOUBLE TO HAVE ON HAND FOR LASAGNES, CANNELLONI OR FOR ADDING EXTRA RICHNESS TO SOUPS OR STEWS.

Fresh tomato and capsicum pasta sauce with lemon ricotta

SERVES 4–6
PREPARATION TIME 15 MINUTES
COOKING TIME 4–4½ HOURS

10 ripe tomatoes

2 tablespoons olive oil

2 red capsicums (peppers), seeds and membranes discarded, cut into 1 cm (½ inch) dice,

2 garlic cloves, crushed

50 g (1¾ oz/¼ cup) red lentils

2 teaspoons fennel seeds

handful basil, leaves coarsely torn, stems finely chopped, plus extra leaves to serve

your choice of pasta, to serve

Lemon ricotta

250 g (9 oz) ricotta cheese

finely grated zest of ½ lemon

Quarter the tomatoes, then remove and discard the seeds using a teaspoon. Coarsely chop the tomatoes.

Put the tomatoes and remaining ingredients into the slow cooker and cook on low for 4 hours, or until the tomatoes and capsicum have broken down into a rich sauce, briefly stirring the sauce once or twice during cooking, if possible.

Just before serving, combine the ricotta and lemon zest and season with sea salt and freshly ground black pepper.

Once cooked, stir the sauce to help it thicken from the lentils. If the sauce is still a bit watery, cook with the lid off for an extra 20–30 minutes. Serve the sauce over pasta, topped with spoonfuls of the lemon ricotta and with the basil leaves scattered over.

Tomato and basil barley risotto

SERVES 4–6
PREPARATION TIME 10 MINUTES (+ SOAKING)
COOKING TIME 3 HOURS

handful fresh basil, leaves and stalks, plus extra to serve

1 litre (35 fl oz/4 cups) good-quality vegetable stock

2 tablespoons olive oil

3 garlic cloves, crushed or finely chopped

6 ripe tomatoes, coarsely chopped

125 ml (4 fl oz/½ cup) white wine (optional)

300 g (10½ oz/1½ cups) barley (soaked, drained and rinsed, see Tip)

20 g (¾ oz) butter

50 g (1¾ oz/½ cup) finely grated parmesan cheese

seed crunch topping (see page 9) (optional)

rocket (arugula) salad, to serve (optional)

Roughly tear half the basil leaves and finely chop all the stalks. Reserve the remaining leaves to serve. Bring the stock to the boil in a small saucepan.

Heat the olive oil in the insert pan of a slow cooker or a frying pan over medium–low heat. Add the garlic, tomatoes, torn basil leaves and chopped stalks and cook, stirring occasionally, for 5 minutes, or until softened and the tomatoes are breaking down. Season well with sea salt and freshly ground black pepper.

Pour in the wine, if using, and stir for 2 minutes, or until it has slightly reduced.

Return the insert pan, if using, to the slow cooker, or transfer the tomato mixture to the slow cooker. Add the barley and hot stock and stir to combine. Cover and cook on high, stirring occasionally, for 3 hours, or until the barley is tender.

Stir the risotto and add a little hot stock or water if the risotto is too thick. Roughly tear the remaining basil leaves and stir into the risotto with the butter and half the parmesan. Serve the risotto with the remaining parmesan and extra basil leaves scattered over and the seed crunch topping, if using. Accompany the dish with a rocket salad, if you like.

TIP To aid digestion, it is advisable to soak the barley in cold water at room temperature for about 6 hours or overnight before using. If you have any, add 2 teaspoons plain yoghurt to help with a little fermentation.

THIS DISH CAN BE SERVED AS A SUBSTANTIAL MEAL ON ITS OWN
BUT IS ALSO GREAT AS PART OF A SPANISH FEAST.

Vegetarian paella

SERVES 4
PREPARATION TIME 20 MINUTES
COOKING TIME 2 HOURS

650 ml (22½ fl oz) good-quality vegetable stock

125 ml (4 fl oz/½ cup) white wine, or extra stock or water

pinch of saffron threads

1 tablespoon olive oil

1 brown onion, finely chopped

2 garlic cloves, crushed or finely chopped

1 red capsicum (pepper), seeds and membranes discarded, coarsely chopped

220 g (7¾ oz/1 cup) paella or arborio rice

½ teaspoon smoked paprika

3 firm, ripe tomatoes, quartered

150 g (5½ oz) green beans, ends trimmed, cut into 1 cm (½ inch) pieces

140 g (5 oz/1 cup) frozen peas, thawed

35 g (1¼ oz/¼ cup) slivered almonds

2 tablespoons finely chopped flat-leaf (Italian) parsley, to serve

1 lemon, cut into wedges, to serve

Bring the stock and wine, if using, to the boil in a small saucepan. Remove from the heat and pour into the slow cooker. Add the saffron threads, put the lid on and turn on to low.

Heat the oil in the same saucepan over medium–high heat and cook the onion and garlic for 5 minutes or until lightly golden.

Add to the slow cooker with the capsicum, rice and paprika. Season well with sea salt and freshly ground black pepper and stir to combine. Scatter the tomatoes over the top. Cook on low for 1 hour 20 minutes or until the rice is almost tender.

Stir in the beans and peas and cook for a further 20 minutes.

Meanwhile, put the almonds into a cold frying pan over medium heat and cook, tossing regularly for 3–4 minutes until lightly golden. Remove from the pan.

Serve the paella with the parsley and almonds scattered over, accompanied by lemon wedges.

Pumpkin and cherry tomato risotto

SERVES 4–6
PREPARATION TIME 15 MINUTES
COOKING TIME 2 HOURS

1.4 litres (49 fl oz) good-quality vegetable stock

1 tablespoon olive oil

1 brown onion, finely chopped

2 garlic cloves, crushed or finely chopped

400 g (14 oz) peeled pumpkin (winter squash) flesh, cut into 1–2 cm (½–¾ inch) dice

440 g (15½ oz/2 cups) arborio rice

200 ml (7 fl oz) white wine, extra stock or water

250 g (9 oz) cherry tomatoes

20 g (¾ oz) butter, chopped

50 g (1¾ oz/½ cup) finely grated parmesan cheese

2 tablespoons coarsely chopped flat-leaf (Italian) parsley, to serve

Bring the stock to the boil in a small saucepan, then remove from the heat.

Heat the oil in the insert pan of a slow cooker or a frying pan over medium–low heat. Add the onion and garlic and cook, stirring, for 3 minutes. Add the pumpkin and cook for 5 minutes.

Return the insert pan, if using, to the slow cooker, or transfer the mixture to the slow cooker. Cover and cook on high, stirring occasionally, for 1 hour.

Add the rice, wine, hot stock and tomatoes. Season with sea salt and freshly ground black pepper and stir to combine. Cover and cook for 35–45 minutes until the rice is tender and most of the liquid has been absorbed.

Stir the butter and three-quarters of the parmesan through the risotto until creamy and combined. Season to taste with sea salt and freshly ground black pepper and serve with the parsley and extra parmesan scattered over.

WARM SALADS AND SIDES

THIS SALAD IS DELICIOUS SCATTERED WITH CRUMBLED FETA CHEESE, WHICH PROVIDES EXTRA CALCIUM. ALTERNATIVELY, IF YOU WANT TO MAKE THIS DISH VEGAN, REPLACE THE BUTTER IN THE COUSCOUS WITH TWO TABLESPOONS OF OLIVE OIL.

Braised root vegetable salad with chickpeas and couscous

SERVES 6
PREPARATION TIME 30 MINUTES
COOKING TIME 3 HOURS 5 MINUTES

400 g (14 oz) cauliflower, cut into large florets

1 large desiree (or other all-purpose) potato, peeled and cut into 3 cm (1¼ inch) chunks

1 sweet potato, peeled, cut into 3 cm (1¼ inch) chunks

1 large beetroot (beet), peeled and cut into 2 cm (¾ inch) wedges

2 carrots, halved lengthways and cut into 3 cm (1¼ inch) chunks

1 whole garlic bulb, cloves separated and peeled

finely grated zest and juice of 1 lemon

60 ml (2 fl oz/¼ cup) extra virgin olive oil

500 ml (17 fl oz/2 cups) good-quality vegetable stock

400 g (14 oz) tin chickpeas, drained and rinsed

240 g (8½ oz/1¼ cups) instant couscous

40 g (1½ oz) butter, at room temperature, chopped

4 tablespoons mint leaves, torn

4 tablespoons coriander (cilantro) leaves, coarsely chopped

25 g (1 oz/¼ cup) flaked almonds, lightly toasted

Place all the vegetables in the slow cooker. Add the garlic and lemon zest. Pour in the olive oil and stock, season with sea salt and freshly ground black pepper and gently mix together. Cover and cook on high for 2½ hours.

Stir in the chickpeas, then cover and cook for a further 30 minutes, or until the vegetables are tender, but still retain some bite.

Carefully pour out the cooking liquid into a large bowl and measure out 310 ml (10¾ fl oz/1¼ cups), making up any difference with extra stock or water. Turn the slow cooker setting to low, then cover and keep cooking the vegetables while preparing the couscous.

Bring the cooking liquid to the boil in a saucepan. Remove from the heat, add the lemon juice and couscous and stir with a fork for 20 seconds. Cover and allow to soften for 5 minutes, then return the saucepan to low heat. Add the butter and fluff the couscous grains with a fork until the butter melts through.

Add the couscous and half the herbs to the slow cooker and gently mix to combine. Spoon onto a large platter, scatter with the remaining herbs and toasted almonds and serve.

TIP For meat eaters, this salad goes well with grilled (broiled) or roasted meats.

PUY LENTILS ARE THE LITTLE BLUE-GREEN ONES THAT, UNLIKE RED LENTILS, RETAIN THEIR SHAPE AND TEXTURE WHEN COOKED. THEY ARE ALSO HIGH IN PROTEIN, RICH IN NUTRIENTS, CHEAP AND EASILY AVAILABLE – WHAT'S NOT TO LOVE?

Warm lentil salad

SERVES 6
PREPARATION TIME 15 MINUTES
COOKING TIME 3½ HOURS

370 g (13 oz/1¾ cups) puy lentils or tiny blue-green lentils

1 teaspoon thyme

2 garlic cloves, halved

finely grated zest of 1 lemon

500 ml (17 fl oz/2 cups) good-quality vegetable stock

Dressing

large handful flat-leaf (Italian) parsley leaves

small handful mint leaves

1 tablespoon salted capers, rinsed

1 medium garlic clove, finely chopped

80 ml (2½ fl oz/⅓ cup) olive oil, plus extra if needed

2 tablespoons lemon juice, plus extra if needed

feta and red chilli crumble topping (see page 11), to serve (optional)

crusty bread, to serve

Pick through the lentils to remove any small stones that might still be present. Rinse the lentils and drain well, then place in the slow cooker with the thyme, garlic and lemon zest. Pour in the stock and 200 ml (7 fl oz) of water. Cover and cook on low for 3½ hours, or until the lentils are soft but not mushy, and all the liquid has been absorbed. If the lentils are cooked but some stock remains, drain it before adding the dressing.

To make the dressing, place the parsley, mint, capers and garlic in a small food processor and blend until combined. With the motor running, slowly add the olive oil and continue processing until emulsified. Stir in the lemon juice.

Add the dressing to the lentils in the slow cooker. Season with sea salt and freshly ground black pepper. Gently mix to combine, adding more lemon juice or olive oil to the lentils if needed to balance the flavour.

Serve with feta and red chilli crumble and crusty bread. Or for meat eaters, with grilled chicken or sausages.

ALOO BHAJI IS A DELICIOUS SPICED POTATO DISH. TRADITIONALLY THE POTATOES ARE FRIED ALONG WITH THE SPICES, BUT COOKING IT SLOWLY PRODUCES SOFTER POTATOES. THIS VERSION ISN'T ESPECIALLY SPICY, SO ADD EXTRA GREEN CHILLIES IF DESIRED.

Aloo bhaji

SERVES 4
PREPARATION TIME 15 MINUTES
COOKING TIME 1 HOUR 10 MINUTES

40 g (1½ oz) ghee

1 kg (2 lb 4 oz) desiree (or other all-purpose) potatoes, peeled and cut into 2.5 cm (1 inch) chunks

2 brown onions, finely chopped

1–2 long green chillies, finely chopped

2 teaspoons finely chopped fresh ginger

½ teaspoon mustard seeds

½ teaspoon ground turmeric

½ teaspoon cumin seeds

1 teaspoon sea salt

2 tablespoons chopped coriander (cilantro) leaves, to garnish

lemon wedges, to serve

Heat the ghee in the insert pan of a slow cooker or a large frying pan over medium–high heat. Add the potato and onion and cook, stirring, for 3–4 minutes until the onion starts to soften.

Stir in the chilli, ginger, spices and salt and cook for a further 2–3 minutes until the potato is golden.

Return the insert pan, if using, to the slow cooker, or transfer the mixture to the slow cooker. Sprinkle 2 tablespoons of water over the mixture, then cover and cook on high for 1 hour, or until the potato is tender.

Garnish with the coriander and serve with lemon wedges.

SERVE THESE MELTINGLY SOFT ONIONS AS AN ACCOMPANIMENT TO ROASTED OR GRILLED MEATS, IF YOU EAT MEAT, OR AS PART OF A FEAST OF VEGETARIAN DISHES.

Slow-cooked onions with thyme and parmesan

SERVES 8–10
PREPARATION TIME 15 MINUTES
COOKING TIME 5 HOURS 10 MINUTES

10 small onions

250 ml (9 fl oz/1 cup) thin (pouring) cream

100 ml (3½ fl oz) good-quality vegetable stock

5 thyme sprigs, plus extra to serve

3 garlic cloves, crushed

30 g (1 oz) butter, chopped

50 g (1¾ oz/½ cup) finely grated parmesan cheese, to serve

Peel the onions, then use a sharp knife to score a cross into the top of each one. Place the onions in a slow cooker, with the scored side facing up.

Pour the cream and stock over the onions, then scatter with the thyme sprigs, garlic and butter. Season with sea salt and freshly ground black pepper. Cover and cook on low, stirring occasionally, for 5 hours.

Carefully strain the cream mixture into a saucepan. Allow to reduce over medium–high heat for 7–10 minutes until the sauce has thickened. Pour the sauce over the onions and season to taste.

Serve sprinkled with the parmesan and extra thyme, if desired.

FENNEL IS A VERY VERSATILE VEGETABLE. IT'S IDEAL FOR SALADS DUE TO ITS CRISP TEXTURE. CONVERSELY, WHEN IT IS COOKED SLOWLY FOR A FEW HOURS, THE BULBS SOFTEN AND THE FLAVOUR SWEETENS.

Braised fennel with sourdough and garlic crumbs

SERVES 6
PREPARATION TIME 15 MINUTES
COOKING TIME 2 HOURS 40 MINUTES

125 ml (4 fl oz/½ cup) olive oil

4 small fennel bulbs, trimmed and cut into 6 wedges

5 thyme sprigs

250 ml (9 fl oz/1 cup) milk

125 ml (4 fl oz/½ cup) good-quality vegetable stock

2 garlic cloves, crushed

125 g (4½ oz/2 cups lightly packed) coarse day-old sourdough breadcrumbs

50 g (1¾ oz/½ cup) finely grated parmesan cheese

Heat 2 tablespoons of the olive oil in the insert pan of a slow cooker or a large frying pan over medium–high heat. Add the fennel and cook, stirring occasionally, for 5–6 minutes until golden.

Return the insert pan, if using, to the slow cooker, or transfer the fennel to the slow cooker. Add the thyme sprigs, milk and stock and season with sea salt and freshly ground black pepper. Cover and cook on high for 2–2½ hours, or until the fennel is very tender.

While the fennel is cooking, heat the remaining oil in a frying pan over medium heat. Add the garlic and breadcrumbs and cook, stirring occasionally, for 2–3 minutes until golden and crisp.

To serve, season the fennel to taste, then sprinkle with the parmesan and the crisp garlic breadcrumbs.

BRIGHTLY COLOURED CAPSICUMS ARE ROBUST VEGETABLES AND SLOW COOKING THEM BRINGS OUT THEIR NATURAL SWEETNESS. ADD TENDER ASPARAGUS AND A HANDFUL OF BASIL AND YOU'VE GOT YOURSELF A DELICIOUS SUMMER SALAD.

Capsicum and asparagus salad with caper dressing

SERVES 4–6
PREPARATION TIME 15 MINUTES
COOKING TIME 2 HOURS 40 MINUTES

- 2 red capsicums (peppers), seeds and membranes discarded, cut into 4–5 cm (1½–2 inch) wide strips
- 2 yellow capsicums (peppers), seeds and membranes discarded, cut into 4–5 cm (1½–2 inch) wide strips
- 80 ml (2½ fl oz/⅓ cup) olive oil
- 2 bunches asparagus, ends trimmed, halved on an angle
- 1 tablespoon sherry vinegar or white wine vinegar
- 1 tablespoon baby capers, rinsed and drained on paper towel
- small handful basil or flat-leaf (Italian) parsley leaves, to serve

Put the capsicum into the slow cooker with 2 tablespoons of the oil. Season with sea salt and freshly ground black pepper and cook on low for 2½ hours.

Add the asparagus, toss gently and cook for a further 10 minutes or until the asparagus is just tender. Take care not to overcook the asparagus and remember the vegetables will continue to cook as they cool down.

While the asparagus is cooking, make the dressing by combining the remaining 2 tablespoons of oil with the vinegar and capers and season with sea salt and freshly ground black pepper.

Transfer the vegetables to a serving platter, leaving the pan juices in the slow cooker, and drizzle over the dressing. Leave to cool to room temperature then scatter with the basil or parsley leaves to serve.

THESE VEGETABLES ARE A GREAT ACCOMPANIMENT TO SO MANY MEALS. THIS DISH IS PARTICULARLY USEFUL IF YOU NEED YOUR OVEN TO COOK OTHER DISHES. THE INGREDIENTS CAN EASILY BE DOUBLED TO SERVE MORE.

Honey-glazed roasted vegetables

SERVES 4
PREPARATION TIME 20 MINUTES
COOKING TIME 3 HOURS

2–3 parsnips (about 400–500 g/14 oz–1 lb 2 oz)

80 ml (2½ fl oz/⅓ cup) olive oil

1 bunch baby carrots, scrubbed or peeled, ends trimmed, left whole or 3 medium carrots cut into batons

600 g (1 lb 5 oz) waxy potatoes, scrubbed and halved (quarter any large ones)

1 red onion, cut into thin wedges

3 thyme sprigs

2 tablespoons honey

1 tablespoon balsamic vinegar

Trim the parsnips and peel. Halve lengthways and remove the core from the top part. Quarter the parsnips if they are particularly large, or leave in halves.

Heat 2 tablespoons of the oil in a large frying pan over medium heat and fry the parsnips, carrots and potatoes (in batches if necessary) for 4–5 minutes until starting to brown. Transfer to the slow cooker with the onion and thyme sprigs.

Combine the remaining oil with the honey and vinegar and pour over the vegetables. Season with sea salt and freshly ground black pepper and toss to combine. Cook on low for 3 hours or until the vegetables are tender.

Transfer to a serving dish, spooning over any pan juices. Season to taste and serve.

THIS FRAGRANT RICE WITH A HINT OF LEMON IS A PERFECT
ACCOMPANIMENT TO INDIAN, MIDDLE EASTERN AND EUROPEAN DISHES.

Herb pilaff with roasted almonds

SERVES 6–8
PREPARATION TIME 20 MINUTES
COOKING TIME 1 HOUR 25 MINUTES

1 tablespoon olive oil

20 g (¾ oz) butter

1 brown onion, diced

3 garlic cloves, finely chopped

500 g (1 lb 2 oz/2½ cups) long-grain white rice

850 ml (29 fl oz) good-quality vegetable stock

1 cinnamon stick

1 preserved lemon quarter

juice of 1 lemon

large handful flat-leaf (Italian) parsley, coarsely torn

large handful mint, coarsely torn

80 g (2¾ oz/½ cup) roasted almonds, coarsely chopped, to garnish

Greek-style yoghurt, to serve

Heat the olive oil and butter in the insert pan of a slow cooker or a frying pan over medium heat. Add the onion and garlic and cook, stirring, for 5–7 minutes until softened.

Return the insert pan, if using, to the slow cooker, or transfer the onion mixture to the slow cooker. Add the rice, stirring to coat the grains in the oil, then add the stock and cinnamon stick. Cover and cook on high, stirring occasionally, for 1–1¼ hours, or until the rice is tender and fluffy, adding a little extra stock or water if the rice seems to be drying out.

Rinse the preserved lemon well, then remove and discard the pulp and membrane. Finely dice the rind, then stir it through the pilaff with the lemon juice and herbs.

Garnish with the almonds and serve with yoghurt.

IF USING DRIED CHICKPEAS THEY WILL NEED TO BE SOAKED OVERNIGHT.
OR YOU CAN USE TINNED CHICKPEAS – RINSE THEM WELL BEFORE
USING AND REDUCE THE INITIAL SLOW COOKING TIME BY ONE HOUR.

Braised chickpeas with onion and silverbeet

SERVES 8–10
PREPARATION TIME 15 MINUTES (+ 8 HOURS SOAKING)
COOKING TIME 4 HOURS 20 MINUTES

375 g (13 oz) dried chickpeas, soaked in cold water for 8 hours or overnight or 2 x 400 g (14 oz) tins chickpeas, drained and rinsed

2 tablespoons olive oil

20 g (¾ oz) butter

1 brown onion, sliced into wedges

4 garlic cloves, crushed

500 g (1 lb 2 oz/½ bunch) silverbeet (Swiss chard), stalks thinly sliced, leaves coarsely chopped, kept separate

1 litre (35 fl oz/4 cups) good-quality vegetable stock

extra virgin olive oil, for drizzling

Drain the chickpeas, discarding the water, then place in a large saucepan. Cover with fresh water and bring to the boil. Boil rapidly for 10 minutes. Rinse the chickpeas and drain again. This cooking is not necessary if using tinned chickpeas.

Meanwhile, heat the olive oil and butter in the insert pan of a slow cooker or a frying pan over medium heat. Add the onion, garlic and silverbeet stalks and cook, stirring, for 5–6 minutes until softened.

Return the insert pan, if using, to the slow cooker, or transfer the mixture to the slow cooker. Add the stock and chickpeas and gently mix together. Cover and cook on high for 3 hours, or until the chickpeas are almost cooked through.

Stir in the silverbeet leaves, then cover and cook for a further 1 hour, or until the chickpeas are very tender.

Season to taste with sea salt and freshly ground black pepper. Serve drizzled with extra virgin olive oil.

THIS IS A TWIST ON THE CLASSIC BOSTON BAKED BEANS, WHICH ARE USUALLY MADE WITH PORK. SMOKED PAPRIKA ADDS SIMILAR DEPTH OF FLAVOUR WITHOUT THE MEAT. THIS MAKES A GREAT BREAKFAST ON BRISK MORNINGS IF YOU GET IT COOKING THE NIGHT BEFORE, BUT IT'S ALSO GREAT FOR DINNER.

Boston beans

SERVES 4
PREPARATION TIME 5 MINUTES (+ OVERNIGHT SOAKING)
COOKING TIME 8¼ HOURS

375 g (13 oz) dried great northern, navy or haricot beans, soaked overnight, drained and rinsed

1 onion, finely chopped

500 ml (17 fl oz/2 cups) good-quality vegetable stock

2 tablespoons maple syrup

2 tablespoons treacle or molasses

1 tablespoon smoked paprika

½ teaspoon cayenne pepper

2 garlic cloves, finely chopped

2 tablespoons dijon mustard

400 g (14 oz) tin chopped tomatoes

1 fresh or dried bay leaf

toasted crusty bread and flat-leaf (Italian) parsley leaves, to serve

Put the beans, onion, stock and 500 ml (17 fl oz/2 cups) of water in a saucepan and bring to the boil. Cook for 10 minutes, skimming any impurities from the surface.

Transfer the contents of the saucepan to the slow cooker. Add the remaining ingredients and cook on low for 8 hours, or until the beans are tender.

Serve with toasted crusty bread and parsley.

YOU SHOULD BE ABLE TO FIND FERMENTED BLACK BEANS AT ASIAN GROCERS AND LARGER SUPERMARKETS. THEIR PUNGENT SALTINESS BRINGS THESE ROOT VEGETABLES TO LIFE.

Parsnips and carrots with black bean sauce

SERVES 4
PREPARATION TIME 5 MINUTES
COOKING TIME 2 HOURS

1 tablespoon sesame oil

80 ml (2½ fl oz/⅓ cup) Chinese rice wine

2 tablespoons fermented black beans, rinsed and coarsely chopped

2 tablespoons finely grated fresh ginger

1½ teaspoons black peppercorns, coarsely ground

2 garlic cloves, crushed

1 teaspoon raw sugar

1 tablespoon tamari or light soy sauce

1 tablespoon malt vinegar

3 parsnips, quartered lengthways and tough cores removed

4 carrots, cut into chunks

sliced spring onion (scallion) and steamed rice, to serve

Combine the sesame oil, rice wine, black beans, ginger, pepper, garlic, sugar, tamari, vinegar and 3 tablespoons of water in the slow cooker.

Add the parsnips and carrots and mix to coat. Cook on high for 2 hours, or until tender.

Serve with spring onion and steamed rice.

THIS MEXICAN-INSPIRED SALAD IS GREAT SERVED WARM OR COLD. CHOOSE YOUR FAVOURITE TOPPING, DEPENDING ON YOUR FAMILY'S PREFERENCES. YOU CAN ALSO DOUBLE THE QUINOA AND STOCK QUANTITIES TO MAKE EXTRA FOR LUNCH THE NEXT DAY.

Quinoa, corn and black bean salad

SERVES 4
PREPARATION TIME 10 MINUTES (OR A LITTLE EXTRA DEPENDING ON TOPPINGS)
COOKING TIME 2 HOURS 50 MINUTES ON LOW, OR 1 HOUR 40 MINUTES ON HIGH

200 g (7 oz/1 cup) quinoa (white or tri-coloured)

500 ml (17 fl oz/2 cups) good-quality vegetable stock

1 teaspoon ground coriander

400 g (14 oz) tin black beans, drained and rinsed

2 corn cobs

60 ml (2 fl oz/¼ cup) olive oil

1 tablespoon sherry vinegar or white wine vinegar

100 g (3½ oz) rocket (arugula) or baby spinach leaves

Toppings (optional)

2 avocados, diced

100 g (3½ oz) goat's cheese or feta cheese

1 long red chilli, thinly sliced

small handful coriander (cilantro) leaves

seed crunch topping (see page 9)

Rinse the quinoa in a sieve under running water. Put it into the slow cooker with the stock, ground coriander and black beans and season well with sea salt and freshly ground black pepper. Cook for 2½ hours on low or 1½ hours on high.

While the quinoa is cooking, put the corn on a board and carefully slice off the kernels.

Add the corn to the quinoa, then drape a tea towel (dish towel) over the slow cooker allowing it to hang over the sides (this absorbs excess moisture). Put the lid on and cook for a further 20 minutes on low or 10 minutes on high or until all the liquid has evaporated. The corn should still have a little crunch to it. Transfer the quinoa mixture to a bowl and let it cool to room temperature.

Whisk together the oil and vinegar and season with sea salt and freshly ground black pepper.

Once the quinoa has cooled, gently fork through it to separate the grains, then stir in the dressing and rocket. Serve with your choice of toppings.

Indian chaat masala cauliflower and spinach

SERVES 4
PREPARATION TIME 10 MINUTES
COOKING TIME 2½–3 HOURS

1 medium cauliflower (about 650–700g/
    1 lb 7 oz–1 lb 9 oz)

1 bunch baby carrots, or 3 medium carrots

2 tablespoons olive oil

1 tablespoon chaat masala (see Tip)

55 g (2 oz/⅓ cup) pepitas (pumpkin seeds)

100 g (3½ oz) baby spinach leaves (or picked
    watercress)

handful flat-leaf (Italian) parsley leaves, coarsely
    torn

150 g (5½ oz) feta cheese

extra virgin olive oil, to serve

lemon halves, for squeezing over

Cut the cauliflower into small florets. If using baby carrots, trim the ends then scrub and halve on an angle. For large carrots, peel and cut into 1 cm (½ inch) slices.

Put the cauliflower and carrots in the slow cooker. Drizzle over the olive oil and scatter over the chaat masala. Season with sea salt and freshly ground black pepper and toss well to coat the vegetables in the spice mixture. Cook on low for 2½–3 hours, or until the vegetables are just tender. Be careful not to overcook them, and remember they will continue to cook while they cool.

While the vegetables are cooking, put the pepitas in a cold small frying pan over medium heat. Toast, tossing regularly for 3–4 minutes. Set aside to cool.

Transfer the cooked vegetables to a large serving dish to cool until warm or at room temperature. Add the spinach leaves, pepitas and parsley and toss to combine. Crumble over the feta and drizzle with extra virgin olive oil and a squeeze of lemon.

TIP Chaat masala is a spice blend commonly used in Indian, Bangladeshi and Pakistani cuisine. One of its main ingredients is amchoor powder (dried mango) which is usually blended with cumin, coriander, ginger and asafoetida. Buy it at Indian grocers.

THIS RECIPE NOT ONLY TASTES GREAT BUT IS A FEAST FOR THE EYES, TOO, THANKS TO THE JEWEL-LIKE COLOURS OF THE BEETROOT. SERVE IT AS A LIGHT MEAL TOPPED WITH GOAT'S CHEESE OR FETA AND ACCOMPANIED BY CRUSTY BREAD OR AS PART OF A SELECTION OF DISHES.

Beetroot, cannellini bean and baby spinach salad

SERVES 4
PREPARATION TIME 15 MINUTES
COOKING TIME 3 HOURS

600–700 g (1 lb 5 oz–1 lb 9 oz) small beetroot (beets) or 3 large beetroot

1 bunch baby carrots, ends trimmed, scrubbed

2 teaspoons fennel seeds

2 tablespoons olive oil

1 red onion, cut into thin wedges

2 x 400 g (14 oz) tins cannellini beans, drained and rinsed

100 g (3½ oz) baby spinach leaves

150 g (5½ oz) goat's cheese or feta cheese (optional)

crusty bread, to serve (optional)

Balsamic dressing

1 tablespoon extra virgin olive oil, plus extra to top up pan juices, if necessary

1 tablespoon balsamic vinegar

Peel the beetroot then cut smaller ones in half and larger ones into wedges.

Put the beetroot, whole carrots and fennel seeds into the slow cooker with the olive oil and onion, season with sea salt and freshly ground black pepper and cook on high for 2½ hours.

Transfer the beetroot and carrots to a serving dish. Carefully pour the pan juices into a small dish and allow to cool. Cool the vegetables for 15 minutes or until cold if serving the salad cold.

For the dressing, measure the pan juices, topping them up to 2 tablespoons with the extra oil if necessary. Combine with the 1 tablespoon of extra virgin olive oil and the balsamic vinegar and season with sea salt and freshly ground black pepper.

Add the beans and spinach to the vegetables and toss gently to combine. Drizzle over the dressing and crumble over your choice of cheese, if using. Serve accompanied by crusty bread, if you like.

BARLEY HAS A LIGHT NUTTY FLAVOUR AND A SLIGHTLY CHEWY TEXTURE AND IS A FANTASTIC GRAIN TO ADD TO A SALAD. TO AID DIGESTION, IT'S ADVISABLE TO SOAK THE BARLEY IN COLD WATER AT ROOM TEMPERATURE FOR ABOUT 6 HOURS BEFORE USING.

Warm barley salad with feta and lemon dressing

SERVES 4
PREPARATION TIME 15 MINUTES (+ SOAKING)
COOKING TIME 6 HOURS ON LOW, OR 3½ HOURS ON HIGH

200 g (7 oz/1 cup) pearl barley (soaked, drained and rinsed) (see Tip)

1 tablespoon olive oil

4 spring onions (scallions), green and white parts thinly sliced, kept separate

1 red capsicum (pepper), seeds and membranes discarded, diced

2 wide strips of lemon peel

750 ml (26 fl oz/3 cups) good-quality vegetable stock

100 g (3½ oz) rocket (arugula)

150 g (5½ oz) feta cheese

seed crunch topping (see page 9)

Lemon dressing

60 ml (2 fl oz/¼ cup) extra virgin olive oil

1 tablespoon lemon juice

Put the barley into the slow cooker with the olive oil, green part of the onions, capsicum, lemon peel and the stock. Season with sea salt and freshly ground black pepper and cook for 6 hours on low or 3½ hours on high.

Once cooked, transfer to a serving dish and allow to cool slightly.

Make the dressing by whisking together the oil and lemon juice and season with sea salt and freshly ground black pepper. Drizzle half the dressing over the barley mixture and toss to combine. Stir through the rocket leaves and crumble over the feta. Serve with the remaining dressing for drizzling over at the table with the white part of the spring onion and seed crunch topping, if you like, scattered over.

TIP If you have any plain yoghurt, add 2 teaspoons to the barley while it's soaking to help with a little fermentation.

ARTICHOKES CAN BE A BIT FIDDLY TO PREPARE, PARTICULARLY THE FIRST TIME, BUT IT'S IMPORTANT TO DO IT PROPERLY. MAKE SURE YOU BUY GLOBE ARTICHOKES AND NOT JERUSALEM ARTICHOKES, WHICH ARE A DIFFERENT VEGETABLE ENTIRELY.

Braised artichokes with potatoes, garlic and sage

SERVES 6–8
PREPARATION TIME 40 MINUTES
COOKING TIME 2½ HOURS

juice of 1 lemon

8 globe artichokes

1 kg (2 lb 4 oz) desiree (or other all-purpose) potatoes, peeled and coarsely chopped into approximately 3 cm (1¼ inch) dice

1 fresh bay leaf

3 garlic cloves

750 ml (26 fl oz/3 cups) good-quality vegetable stock

1 tablespoon sage, coarsely chopped

olive oil, for shallow frying

small handful sage leaves, to serve

extra virgin olive oil, for drizzling

Add the lemon juice to a bowl of water. Using a large knife, cut off and discard the top 4–5 cm (1½–2 inches) of each artichoke. Cut off the stalks, leaving 4–5 cm intact. Remove and discard most of the tough outer leaves until you reach the softer inner leaves. Cut each artichoke into quarters and scrape away the hairy choke inside. As you're working, add the artichoke quarters to the lemon water so they don't discolour.

Drain the artichokes and place in the slow cooker with the potato, bay leaf and whole, peeled garlic. Pour in enough stock to just cover the vegetables. Cover and cook on high for 2–2½ hours, stirring occasionally, until the artichokes and potatoes are tender. Stir in the chopped sage during the last 30 minutes of cooking.

Once the chopped sage has been added, heat 1–2 cm (½–¾ inch) of olive oil in a small frying pan over medium–high heat and fry the sage leaves for about 30 seconds until crisp. Drain on paper towel.

Transfer the vegetables to a warm serving dish using a slotted spoon. Drizzle with a little of the braising liquid and some extra virgin olive oil. Season to taste with sea salt and freshly ground black pepper and serve with the fried sage leaves scattered over.

DESSERTS

THIS GLUTEN-FREE CAKE WAS MADE IN A 5.5 LITRE (192 FL OZ/22 CUP) SLOW COOKER. IF YOUR SLOW COOKER IS LARGER OR SMALLER THAN THIS, THE COOKING TIME MAY VARY, SO KEEP AN EYE ON YOUR CAKE FOR THE LAST HOUR OR SO.

Orange and poppy seed cake

SERVES 8
PREPARATION TIME 10 MINUTES
COOKING TIME 3 HOURS (+ 30 MINUTES RESTING)

200 g (7 oz/2 cups) almond meal (ground almonds)

120 g (4¼ oz/1 cup) quinoa flour

2½ teaspoons baking powder

4 tablespoons poppy seeds

finely grated zest and juice of 2 oranges – you need 250 ml (9 fl oz/1 cup) juice

125 ml (4 fl oz/½ cup) light olive oil, plus extra for greasing

130 g (4¾ oz/½ cup) Greek-style yoghurt

185 ml (6 fl oz/¾ cup) honey

1 teaspoon natural vanilla extract

3 eggs, lightly beaten

Candied oranges and syrup

juice of 1 large orange

4 tablespoons honey

1 large orange, thinly sliced

Grease the slow cooker and line with baking paper. Lay a clean tea towel (dish towel) on the bench and place the lid of the slow cooker onto the towel. Pull the towel up over the lid, securing the corners around the knob with string or an elastic band – this is to catch condensation, preventing it from dripping onto the cake as it cooks.

Combine the almond meal, flour, baking powder and poppy seeds in a large bowl.

In another bowl, whisk together the orange zest and juice, oil, yoghurt, honey, vanilla and eggs, then gradually whisk into the almond meal mixture to make a batter.

Pour the cake batter into the slow cooker and cook on low for 3 hours, or until a skewer inserted into the centre comes out clean. Turn off the slow cooker but leave the cake in it for another 30 minutes.

Meanwhile, for the candied oranges and syrup, put the orange juice and honey in a small, non-reactive saucepan. Bring to the boil, then reduce the heat to medium. Add the orange slices and cook for 5 minutes each side until the slices shrink and caramelise.

Carefully remove the cake and top with the candied oranges and syrup.

TO MAKE THIS DESSERT COMPLETELY DAIRY-FREE, DRIZZLE WITH
COCONUT CREAM INSTEAD OF SERVING WITH MASCARPONE.

Apple and blueberry pie

SERVES 8
PREPARATION TIME 15 MINUTES
COOKING TIME 2½ HOURS (+ 30 MINUTES RESTING)

1 kg (2 lb 4 oz) granny smith apples, peeled, quartered, cores removed, cut into very thin slices

1 teaspoon mixed spice

3 eggs

155 g (5½ oz/1 cup) coconut sugar

250 ml (9 fl oz/1 cup) melted coconut oil, plus extra for greasing

3 tablespoons agave syrup or mild honey

1 vanilla bean, split lengthways, seeds scraped

150 g (5½ oz/1 cup) plain (all-purpose) flour, sifted

125 g (4½ oz) fresh or frozen blueberries

mascarpone, to serve

Lightly grease the slow cooker. In a bowl, combine the apples with the mixed spice, then evenly layer them in the slow cooker.

Using an electric mixer, beat the eggs and sugar until pale and thick, then beat in the coconut oil, syrup and vanilla seeds until combined. Using a spatula or large metal spoon, gently fold in the flour, followed by the blueberries.

Pour the batter over the apples to cover. Cook on high for 2½ hours, then turn off the slow cooker and set aside for 30 minutes before removing.

Serve with mascarpone.

Apple, rhubarb and strawberry cobbler

SERVES 6
PREPARATION TIME 25 MINUTES
COOKING TIME 3¾ HOURS

330 g (11½ oz/1½ cups) white granulated sugar

1 teaspoon ground cinnamon

1 vanilla bean, split lengthways, seeds scraped

1 kg (2 lb 4 oz) granny smith apples, peeled, cored and cut into 3 cm (1¼ inch) chunks

500 g (1 lb 2 oz) rhubarb, trimmed and cut into 3 cm (1¼ inch) lengths

250 g (9 oz) strawberries, hulled and halved

2 teaspoons lemon juice

Batter

150 g (5½ oz/1 cup) plain (all-purpose) flour

1½ teaspoons baking powder

55 g (2 oz/¼ cup) white granulated sugar

60 g (2¼ oz) unsalted butter, chopped and slightly softened

125 ml (4 fl oz/½ cup) milk

1 teaspoon natural vanilla extract

2 tablespoons cornflour (cornstarch)

Place the sugar, cinnamon and vanilla seeds in a large bowl and mix to combine. Add the apple, rhubarb and strawberries and toss to combine.

Transfer the mixture to the slow cooker, adding the scraped vanilla bean. Drizzle over the lemon juice and 125 ml (4 fl oz/½ cup) of water. Cover and cook on low for 2½ hours.

To make the batter, sift the flour and baking powder into a bowl, add the sugar and mix to combine. Work in the butter using your fingertips until combined. Stir in the milk and vanilla until just smooth.

Blend the cornflour with 2 tablespoons of water until smooth. Working as quickly as possible, so the slow cooker doesn't lose too much heat, remove the lid and stir the cornflour mixture through the fruit. Quickly dollop the batter over the top, using a large spoon.

Cover and cook on high for 1¼ hours, or until the batter is cooked. Serve warm.

YES, YOU CAN EVEN COOK BROWNIES IN YOUR SLOW COOKER! THESE BROWNIES USE THREE DIFFERENT TYPES OF CHOCOLATE AND WILL HAVE EVERY CHOCOLATE FAN BEGGING FOR MORE.

Triple chocolate brownies

MAKES 12
PREPARATION TIME 15 MINUTES
COOKING TIME 2½ HOURS (+ 20 MINUTES RESTING)

225 g (8 oz/1 cup) coconut oil, plus extra for greasing

200 g (7 oz) dark 70% chocolate, chopped

3 tablespoons cacao powder, plus extra for dusting

125 ml (4 fl oz/½ cup) maple syrup

80 ml (2½ fl oz/⅓ cup) agave syrup or mild honey

1 teaspoon natural vanilla extract

3 eggs, lightly beaten

¼ teaspoon salt

150 g (5½ oz/1 cup) wholemeal (whole-wheat) plain (all-purpose) flour

1 teaspoon baking powder

3 tablespoons coarsely chopped walnuts

75 g (2¾ oz) good-quality milk chocolate, cut into 1 cm (½ inch) pieces

Grease the slow cooker and line with baking paper. Melt the coconut oil and dark chocolate in a heatproof bowl set over a saucepan of barely simmering water.

Once melted, stir in the cacao powder, maple syrup, agave syrup, vanilla, eggs and salt. Fold in the flour and baking powder until just combined, then stir in the walnuts and milk chocolate.

Pour into the slow cooker (see Tip) and cook on low for 2½ hours or until cooked through when you poke a skewer into the centre and a few crumbs stick. Turn off the slow cooker, leaving the brownie inside for 20 minutes, then remove to prevent the brownie overcooking.

Use the baking paper to gently lift out the brownie and cut it into pieces. Dust with cacao powder to serve.

TIP We used a large, wide-based 6 litre (210 fl oz/24 cup) slow cooker to make these. If yours is a different size or shape the cooking time may vary, so test the brownies with a skewer a few times during the last half hour.

Chai-spiced poached pears

SERVES 4
PREPARATION TIME 5 MINUTES (+ 15 MINUTES STEEPING)
COOKING TIME 3½ HOURS

155 g (5½ oz/1 cup) coconut sugar

3 tablespoons honey

4 cm (1½ inch) piece fresh ginger, thinly sliced

6 cardamom pods, cracked

2 cinnamon sticks, broken in half

8 cloves

1 teaspoon black peppercorns

4 black tea bags

4 firm pears, such as beurre bosc, halved, cores
   removed

vanilla ice cream and toasted pistachios, to serve

Put the sugar, honey, ginger and spices into the slow cooker.
Pour in 1.5 litres (52 fl oz/6 cups) of boiling water and stir well
to dissolve the sugar. Add the tea bags and leave to steep
for 15 minutes. Remove the tea bags and discard.

Add the pears to the slow cooker. Cut out a piece of baking
paper to fit the slow cooker and lay it directly on the surface of
the liquid. Cook on low for about 3½ hours until the pears are
tender – the exact cooking time will depend on their ripeness.

Serve the pears hot, cold or at room temperature with vanilla
ice cream and toasted pistachios.

THIS CHEESECAKE KEEPS WELL FOR A FEW DAYS IN THE FRIDGE, AND
THE BASE BECOMES EXTRA GOOEY AND DELICIOUS AS IT SITS. PERFECT
WITH A MID-MORNING OR AFTER-DINNER ESPRESSO.

Pumpkin and cinnamon cheesecake

SERVES 8–10
PREPARATION TIME 25 MINUTES
COOKING TIME 6 HOURS 10 MINUTES (+ 30 MINUTES RESTING)

400 g (14 oz) peeled and seeded jap or kent
   pumpkin, cut into 4 cm (1½ inch) cubes

150 g (5½ oz/1 cup) plain (all-purpose) flour

½ teaspoon baking powder

4 eggs

155 g (5½ oz/1 cup) coconut sugar

150 g (5½ oz) unsalted butter, melted, plus
   extra for greasing

250 g (9 oz) cream cheese, softened

125 ml (4 fl oz/½ cup) maple syrup

2 teaspoons natural vanilla extract

2 teaspoons ground cinnamon

Cook the pumpkin in a saucepan of boiling water for
10 minutes until tender. Drain in a colander and leave to air-dry.

Meanwhile, sift the flour and baking powder into a bowl.
Lightly beat one of the eggs and add to the flour with half
the sugar and 50 g (1¾ oz) of the melted butter and mix until
a dough forms.

Grease the slow cooker and line with baking paper. Press the
dough evenly over the base of the slow cooker.

Transfer the pumpkin to a bowl, and purée it using a stick
blender, food processor or blender. Add the cream cheese,
maple syrup, vanilla and cinnamon, plus the remaining sugar,
and process until smooth. Add the remaining 3 eggs, one at
a time, pulsing after each addition until combined. Add the
remaining butter and pulse again.

Pour the cheesecake mixture into the slow cooker and cook on
low for 6 hours, or until just set – the centre should still wobble
slightly. Turn off the slow cooker and leave the cheesecake to
rest for 30 minutes before removing.

Set aside to cool completely.

IS THERE ANYTHING BETTER THAN A WARMING RICE PUDDING?
THIS SIMPLE DESSERT USES COCONUT MILK AS WELL AS MILK
FOR ADDED RICHNESS.

Coconut rice pudding

SERVES 6
PREPARATION TIME 10 MINUTES
COOKING TIME 4 HOURS

625 ml (21½ fl oz/2½ cups) coconut milk

625 ml (21½ fl oz/2½ cups) milk

110 g (3¾ oz/½ cup) caster (superfine) sugar

6 kaffir lime leaves

220 g (7¾ oz/1 cup) medium-grain white rice

grated palm sugar (jaggery) or brown sugar, for
 sprinkling

Place the coconut milk, milk, sugar, lime leaves and rice in the slow cooker and gently mix together. Cover and cook on low for 4 hours.

Serve warm, sprinkled with palm sugar or brown sugar.

TIP In warmer months, this dish is delicious served cold with some sliced fresh mango.

IF YOU CAN'T FIND A FRUIT LOAF, THIS BREAD AND BUTTER PUDDING
IS ALSO GREAT WITH SLICED CROISSANTS, HOT CROSS BUNS
OR A CRUSTY WHITE LOAF.

Marmalade bread and butter pudding

SERVES 8
PREPARATION TIME 20 MINUTES
COOKING TIME 4 HOURS

600 g (1 lb 5 oz) thickly sliced fruit loaf, with the crust on

60 g (2¼ oz) butter, softened, plus extra for greasing

225 g (8 oz/⅔ cup) good-quality marmalade, plus an extra 115 g (4 oz/⅓ cup), for brushing (see Tip)

6 eggs

165 g (5¾ oz/¾ cup) white granulated sugar, plus an extra 1½ teaspoons, for sprinkling

250 ml (9 fl oz/1 cup) milk

500 ml (17 fl oz/2 cups) thin (pouring) cream

2 teaspoons natural vanilla extract

vanilla ice cream, to serve

Spread half the fruit loaf slices with the butter, then spread the remaining slices with the marmalade. Sandwich together and cut in half on the diagonal.

Grease the slow cooker and arrange the bread slices inside it on a slight angle, covering the base.

In a bowl, whisk together the eggs, sugar, milk, cream and vanilla. Pour over the bread and gently press the bread down with your hands to help the liquid soak into the bread.

Sprinkle with the extra sugar. Cover and cook on low for 4 hours.

Brush the pudding with the extra marmalade and serve warm, with vanilla ice cream.

TIP It's good to use marmalade with citrus zest in it, or even a bitter English-style marmalade, as a contrast to the sweetness of this dish.

Sago pudding with caramelised pineapple

SERVES 6
PREPARATION TIME 20 MINUTES
COOKING TIME 3 HOURS

100 g (3½ oz/½ cup) sago or tapioca pearls

100 g (3½ oz/½ cup lightly packed) brown sugar

¼ teaspoon ground cinnamon

½ teaspoon natural vanilla extract

finely grated zest of 1 lemon

400 ml (14 fl oz) milk

2 x 400 ml (14 fl oz) tins coconut milk, shaken

2 egg yolks

20 g (¾ oz) butter or ghee

160 g (5¾ oz/1 cup) chopped fresh pineapple pieces

25 g (1 oz/⅓ cup) shredded coconut, lightly toasted

Place the sago in the slow cooker with 2 tablespoons of the sugar, the cinnamon, vanilla, lemon zest and a pinch of salt. Pour in the milk and coconut milk and gently mix together.

Cover and cook on low for 2–2½ hours, or until the sago is tender, stirring once during cooking.

In a bowl, whisk the egg yolks with 2 tablespoons of the remaining sugar until thick. Slowly whisk 250 ml (9 fl oz/1 cup) of the hot sago mixture into the eggs until well combined. Pour the egg mixture back into the slow cooker and stir well to combine. Cover and cook for a further 15–20 minutes until thickened.

Meanwhile, melt the butter in a frying pan over medium heat. Add the pineapple pieces and cook for 2–3 minutes until the pineapple starts to release its juice. Increase the heat to medium–high, sprinkle with the remaining 2 tablespoons of sugar and cook for a further 4–5 minutes, shaking the pan until the pineapple is lightly caramelised. Transfer the pineapple and syrup to a bowl.

Serve the pudding immediately, topped with the pineapple, syrup and coconut.

A GLUTEN- AND DAIRY-FREE DESSERT FOR EVERYONE TO ENJOY.
IF YOU'RE NOT AVOIDING DAIRY, FEEL FREE TO SERVE THIS WITH
CREAM OR ICE CREAM.

Honey rhubarb nut crumble

SERVES 6
PREPARATION TIME 5 MINUTES
COOKING TIME 2 HOURS

155 g (5½ oz/1 cup) macadamia nuts

1 kg (2 lb 4 oz) rhubarb (approximately 2 bunches) trimmed, cut into 5 cm (2 inch) pieces

125 ml (4 fl oz/½ cup) honey

2 teaspoons natural vanilla extract

1 teaspoon ground ginger

1 teaspoon ground cinnamon

125 ml (4 fl oz/½ cup) melted coconut oil, plus extra for greasing

100 g (3½ oz/1 cup) almond meal (ground almonds)

155 g (5½ oz/1 cup) blanched almonds

80 g (2¾ oz/⅔ cup) walnuts, toasted and coarsely chopped

cream or ice cream, to serve (optional)

Put the macadamia nuts in a cold frying pan over medium heat. Toast, tossing, for 3–4 minutes until evenly golden. Remove from the heat. Allow to cool slightly, then coarsely chop.

Lightly oil the slow cooker. Combine the rhubarb, 80 ml (2½ fl oz/⅓ cup) of the honey, the vanilla, ginger and cinnamon in the slow cooker.

In a bowl, combine the remaining ingredients, including the rest of the honey, and scatter over the rhubarb mixture. Cook the crumble on high for 2 hours.

SLOW COOKING SUITS QUINCES WELL, BECAUSE THE
LONGER AND SLOWER THEY ARE COOKED THE MORE THEIR
FLAVOUR INTENSIFIES AND THEY TURN A BEAUTIFUL PINK.

Poached quinces with cinnamon custard

SERVES 8–10
PREPARATION TIME 20 MINUTES (+ 30 MINUTES INFUSING)
COOKING TIME 8 HOURS 10 MINUTES

1 kg (2 lb 4 oz) caster (superfine) sugar

2 cinnamon sticks

2 star anise

1 vanilla bean, split lengthways, seeds scraped

juice of 1 lemon

6 quinces

40 g (1½ oz/⅓ cup) toasted pistachio nuts, coarsely chopped

Cinnamon custard

500 ml (17 fl oz/2 cups) milk

400 ml (14 fl oz) thin (pouring) cream

1 teaspoon ground cinnamon

6 egg yolks

150 g (5½ oz/¾ cup) raw caster (superfine) sugar

Place the sugar, cinnamon sticks, star anise and vanilla bean and seeds in the insert pan of a slow cooker or a saucepan. Pour in 1.2 litres (42 fl oz) of water. Bring to a simmer over medium–high heat, stirring occasionally, for 5–7 minutes until the sugar has dissolved. Return the insert pan, if using, to the slow cooker, or transfer the syrup to the slow cooker.

Meanwhile, add the lemon juice to a bowl of water. Peel, core and quarter the quinces, adding them to the lemon water to prevent browning. Place the quince cores and peel in a piece of muslin (cheesecloth), gather the ends and tie them together to form a pouch. Add the pouch to the syrup. Drain the quince and add to the syrup. Cover and cook on low for 7–8 hours, or until the quince is tender. Remove the muslin pouch.

About 45 minutes before serving time, make the cinnamon custard. Combine the milk, cream and cinnamon in a saucepan over medium heat. Bring just to the boil, then set aside to infuse for 30 minutes. Whisk together the egg yolks and sugar. Bring the milk mixture back to just below a simmer. Slowly pour the egg yolk mixture into the milk mixture, whisking continuously to combine. Transfer the custard to a clean saucepan and cook over medium heat, stirring continuously, for 5–7 minutes until the custard thickly coats the back of a wooden spoon. Remove from the heat and stir until just warm. Cover and keep warm.

Serve the quince with the cinnamon custard, and sprinkled with the pistachios.

THINKING ABOUT WHAT TO SERVE FOR DESSERT OFTEN TAKES SECOND PLACE TO THE MAIN COURSE. PUT THESE ON IN THE MORNING AND THEN FORGET ABOUT THEM UNTIL THE FAMILY ASKS 'WHAT'S FOR DESSERT?'

Stuffed apples with vanilla cream

SERVES 4
PREPARATION TIME 20 MINUTES
COOKING TIME 6 HOURS

1 tablespoon desiccated coconut

4 granny smith apples, about 200 g (7 oz) each

60 g (2¼ oz/⅓ cup lightly packed) brown sugar

60 g (2¼ oz/⅓ cup) raisins, coarsely chopped

2 tablespoons chopped walnuts

½ teaspoon ground cinnamon, plus extra to serve

¼ teaspoon ground ginger

pinch of ground cloves

1 tablespoon honey

185 ml (6 fl oz/¾ cup) thick (double) cream

¼ teaspoon freshly grated nutmeg

20 g (¾ oz) unsalted butter, plus extra for greasing

Lightly grease the base of the slow cooker and sprinkle with the coconut.

Core the apples, leaving the bases intact, then slice the bottom off each one so it sits flat. Make a small incision in the skin around the middle of each apple to allow steam to escape during cooking. Peel off a 1 cm (½ inch) ring from around the top of each apple.

In a bowl, mix together the sugar, raisins, walnuts, cinnamon, ginger, cloves and honey. Pack the mixture into the middle of each apple where the core has been removed. Place the apples in the slow cooker, pour the cream over them and dust the tops with nutmeg. Dot the apples with the butter.

Cover and cook on low for 6 hours, or until the apples are tender but not mushy.

Carefully remove each apple to a warm bowl. Stir the cream sauce to recombine it, then pour over the apples. Serve warm, sprinkled with extra cinnamon.

Rice pudding with baked strawberries and rhubarb

SERVES 6
PREPARATION TIME 20 MINUTES
COOKING TIME 1 HOUR 40 MINUTES

750 ml (26 fl oz/3 cups) milk

250 ml (9 fl oz/1 cup) thin (pouring) cream

140 g (5 oz/⅔ cups) raw caster (superfine) sugar

1 cinnamon stick

½ vanilla bean, split in half lengthways, seeds scraped

220 g (7¾ oz/1 cup) white short-grain or medium-grain rice

3 egg yolks

20 g (¾ oz) butter, chopped

Baked strawberries and rhubarb

750 g (1 lb 10 oz) rhubarb, trimmed and cut into 4 cm (1½ inch) lengths

250 g (9 oz) strawberries, hulled and halved

90 g (3¼ oz/½ cup) raw caster (superfine) sugar

juice of ½ orange

½ vanilla bean, split lengthways, seeds scraped

Combine the milk, cream, sugar, cinnamon stick and the vanilla bean and seeds in the insert pan of a slow cooker or in a saucepan. Bring to a simmer over medium heat.

Return the insert pan, if using, to the slow cooker, or transfer the mixture to the slow cooker. Stir in the rice, then cover and cook on high for 1–1½ hours, or until the rice is tender.

Meanwhile, bake the rhubarb and strawberries. Preheat the oven to 180°C (350°F). Combine the rhubarb, strawberries, sugar, orange juice and the vanilla bean and seeds in a baking dish. Cover with foil and roast for 15–20 minutes, stirring once, until the rhubarb is tender. Remove the vanilla bean.

Remove the vanilla bean from the rice pudding, then stir the egg yolks and butter through until well combined. Top with the baked rhubarb and strawberries and serve.

POACHED PEARS ARE IDEAL WINTER WARMING FOOD. THEY ARE RIDICULOUSLY EASY TO MAKE, TASTE DELICIOUS AND LOOK STUNNING. ALTERNATIVELY, COOL THE POACHING LIQUID, CHILL THE PEARS AND SERVE COLD FOR A BEAUTIFUL SUMMER DESSERT.

Pears poached in ginger wine

SERVES 6
PREPARATION TIME 15 MINUTES
COOKING TIME 3 HOURS

750 ml (26 fl oz/3 cups) green ginger wine

660 g (1 lb 7 oz/3 cups) caster (superfine) sugar

1 lime

6 beurre bosc pears, peeled, with the stems left intact

vanilla ice cream, to serve

Pour the ginger wine and 750 ml (26 fl oz/3 cups) of water into the slow cooker. Stir in the sugar.

Remove thick strips of zest from the lime using a vegetable peeler, being careful to avoid the bitter white pith. Squeeze and strain the juice from the lime and add it to the slow cooker with the zest strips.

Add the pears to the liquid (they will float). Cut a piece of baking paper the size of your slow cooker and lay it directly on the pears. Cover and cook on high for 3 hours, or until the pears are tender.

Serve warm with a scoop of vanilla ice cream, drizzled with some of the syrup.

TIP You could make the dessert more substantial by serving the pears with some sponge cake and sprinkled with chopped pistachio nuts.

Self-saucing dark chocolate fig and hazelnut pudding

SERVES 6–8
PREPARATION TIME 10 MINUTES
COOKING TIME 2 HOURS

55g (2 oz/⅓ cup) blanched hazelnuts

125 ml (4 fl oz/½ cup) melted butter, plus extra for greasing

235 g (8½ oz/1½ cups) coconut sugar

225 g (8 oz/1½ cups) self-raising flour, sifted

1 egg, lightly beaten

250 ml (9 fl oz/1 cup) almond milk

2 teaspoons natural vanilla extract

55 g (2 oz/½ cup) cacao powder

6 dried figs, coarsely chopped

100 g (3½ oz) dark chocolate, coarsely chopped

cream, ice cream or crème fraîche, to serve

Put the hazelnuts in a cold frying pan over medium heat. Toast, tossing, for 3–4 minutes until evenly golden. Remove from the heat. Allow to cool slightly, then coarsely chop.

Lightly grease the slow cooker. In a bowl, combine the melted butter, 155 g (5½ oz/1 cup) of the coconut sugar, the flour, egg, milk, vanilla and 3 tablespoons of the cacao.

Fold in the figs, chocolate and 3 tablespoons of the hazelnuts, then spoon into the slow cooker, spreading the mixture out evenly. Scatter with the remaining sugar, cacao and hazelnuts.

Gently pour over 625 ml (21½ fl oz/2½ cups) of boiling water and cook on low for 2 hours or until set, then serve, accompanied by your choice of cream, ice cream or crème fraîche.

WHO CAN RESIST A CLASSIC STICKY DATE PUDDING? YOU NEED
A SMALL SLOW COOKER FOR THIS, WITH A CAPACITY NO GREATER
THAN 4 LITRES (140 FL OZ/16 CUPS).

Sticky date pudding

SERVES 8
PREPARATION TIME 10 MINUTES (+ 20 MINUTES SOAKING)
COOKING TIME 3 HOURS

240 g (8½ oz/1½ cups) pitted dates, coarsely
chopped

1 teaspoon bicarbonate of soda (baking soda)

80 g (2¾ oz) butter, plus extra for greasing

80 g (2¾ oz/½ cup) coconut sugar

80 ml (2½ fl oz/⅓ cup) maple syrup

80 ml (2½ fl oz/⅓ cup) light olive oil

2 eggs

225 g (8 oz/1½ cups) self-raising flour

vanilla ice cream, to serve

Caramel sauce

125 ml (4 fl oz/½ cup) maple syrup

80 g (2¾ oz/½ cup) coconut sugar

100 g (3½ oz) butter

¼ teaspoon salt

Grease the slow cooker and line with baking paper. Put the
dates and bicarbonate of soda into a heatproof bowl. Pour
over 375 ml (13 fl oz/1½ cups) of boiling water and set aside
for 20 minutes.

Using an electric mixer, beat the butter, sugar and maple syrup
until thick and pale. Beat in the oil, then add the eggs one at
a time, beating well after each addition. Gently fold in the date
mixture, followed by the flour, until just combined. Spoon into
the slow cooker and cook on low for 3 hours.

To make the caramel sauce, put the maple syrup and sugar into
a small saucepan over medium heat, stirring until dissolved.
Add the butter and salt, stirring to melt. Once the butter has
melted, reduce the heat to low and cook for 5 minutes until
thickened slightly.

Carefully remove the pudding and serve with the caramel
sauce and ice cream.

Coconut brown rice pudding with banana and ginger

SERVES 4
PREPARATION TIME 5 MINUTES
COOKING TIME 5 HOURS

220 g (7¾ oz/1 cup) medium-grain brown rice

400 ml (14 fl oz) tin coconut milk, shaken

750 ml (26 fl oz/3 cups) rice or almond milk

4 tablespoons coarsely grated dark palm sugar (jaggery)

1 tablespoon finely grated fresh ginger

2 bananas, chopped

4 kaffir lime leaves

¼ teaspoon salt

sliced banana, black sesame seeds, very finely shredded kaffir lime leaves, shredded coconut and sliced glacé ginger, to serve

Put all the ingredients into the slow cooker and cook on low for 5 hours, or until the rice is tender.

Serve with banana, black sesame seeds, shredded kaffir lime leaves, shredded coconut and glacé ginger.

THIS IS A VERY SIMPLE DESSERT TO MAKE. THE CHOCOLATE TOPPING
AND WATER GRADUALLY SEEP INTO THE BATTER AS IT COOKS,
RESULTING IN GOOEY CHOCOLATE HEAVEN!

Gooey chocolate and hazelnut pudding

SERVES 8–10
PREPARATION TIME 20 MINUTES
COOKING TIME 2 HOURS

75 g (2¾ oz/½ cup) blanched hazelnuts

250 g (9 oz/1⅔ cups) plain (all-purpose) flour

250 g (9 oz/1⅓ cups) raw caster (superfine) sugar

1 tablespoon baking powder

55 g (2 oz/½ cup) unsweetened cocoa powder

500 ml (17 fl oz/2 cups) milk

180 g (6 oz) butter, melted

4 eggs, lightly beaten

150 g (5½ oz/1 cup) coarsely chopped dark chocolate

vanilla or hazelnut ice cream, to serve

Topping

200 g (7 oz) brown sugar

30 g (1 oz/¼ cup) unsweetened cocoa powder

Put the hazelnuts in a cold frying pan over medium heat. Toast, tossing for 3–4 minutes until evenly golden. Remove from the heat. Allow to cool slightly, then coarsely chop.

Sift the flour, sugar, baking powder, cocoa powder and a pinch of salt into a bowl. Add the milk, butter and eggs and stir until smooth. Fold the chocolate and hazelnuts through, then pour the batter into the slow cooker.

Combine the topping ingredients in a bowl, then sprinkle over the pudding batter. Pour 400 ml (14 fl oz) of hot water over the top. Cover and cook on high for 2 hours, or until the pudding is just cooked through but is still a little gooey.

Serve with vanilla or hazelnut ice cream.

TIP We used a 5 litre (175 fl oz/20 cup) slow cooker to make this pudding. If yours is a different size, the cooking time may vary.

Bread, peanut butter and jam pudding

SERVES 6
PREPARATION TIME 15 MINUTES (+ 15 MINUTES SOAKING)
COOKING TIME 3–3½ HOURS

90 g (3¼ oz/⅓ cup) crunchy peanut butter

165 g (5¾ oz/½ cup) raspberry jam

8 thick sourdough bread slices, cut in half diagonally

6 eggs

500 ml (17 fl oz/2 cups) milk

125 ml (4 fl oz/½ cup) thin (pouring) cream

80 g (2¾ oz/½ cup) coconut sugar

1 teaspoon natural vanilla extract

Lightly spread the peanut butter and half the jam over both sides of the bread slices, then arrange in the slow cooker.

Whisk the eggs, milk, cream, sugar and vanilla in a jug or bowl until the sugar dissolves. Pour into the slow cooker, pressing down the bread slices to submerge them. Set aside to soak for 15 minutes.

Cook on low for 3–3½ hours until set.

In a small bowl, combine the remaining jam with 1 tablespoon of boiling water. Serve the pudding drizzled with this jam syrup.

THIS IS A LIGHT AND FLUFFY DESSERT, GREAT IN BOTH SUMMER AND WINTER WHEN YOU DON'T WANT SOMETHING HEAVY AT THE END OF A MEAL. THE FLUFFINESS IS ACHIEVED BY WHISKING THE EGG WHITES BEFORE ADDING THEM TO THE BATTER.

Lemon pudding

SERVES 4
PREPARATION TIME 15 MINUTES (+ 10 MINUTES COOLING)
COOKING TIME 2 HOURS 35 MINUTES

60 g (2¼ oz) unsalted butter, chopped, plus some softened butter for greasing

3 eggs, separated

165 g (5¾ oz/¾ cup) white granulated or caster (superfine) sugar

finely grated zest of 1 lemon

60 ml (2 fl oz/¼ cup) strained lemon juice

375 ml (13 fl oz/1½ cups) milk

35 g (1¼ oz/¼ cup) plain (all-purpose) flour

ice cream, to serve

Melt the butter in a very small saucepan over low heat. Set aside to cool for 10 minutes.

Meanwhile, grease the slow cooker with the softened butter.

Place the egg yolks, sugar, lemon zest and lemon juice in a large bowl. Beat until combined, using electric beaters. Add the melted butter and beat until combined, then add the milk and beat until combined. Beat in the flour.

Using clean electric beaters and a clean bowl, beat the egg whites until stiff peaks form. Gently fold the egg whites through the lemon mixture.

Pour the batter into the slow cooker. Lay a clean tea towel (dish towel) on the bench and place the lid of the slow cooker onto the towel. Pull the towel up over the lid, securing the corners around the knob with string or an elastic band – this is to catch any condensation, preventing it from dripping onto the pudding as it cooks. Place the lid on the slow cooker and cook on low for 2½ hours, or until the pudding is set. Serve warm, with ice cream.

TIP We used a 5 litre (175 fl oz/20 cup) slow cooker to make this pudding. If yours is a different size, the cooking time may vary.

Index

Published in 2018 by Murdoch Books,
an imprint of Allen & Unwin

Murdoch Books Australia
83 Alexander Street
Crows Nest NSW 2065
Phone: +61 (0) 2 8425 0100
Fax: +61 (0) 2 9906 2218
murdochbooks.com.au
info@murdochbooks.com.au

Murdoch Books UK
Ormond House
26–27 Boswell Street
London WC1N 3JZ
Phone: +44 (0) 20 8785 5995
murdochbooks.co.uk
info@murdochbooks.co.uk

For Corporate Orders & Custom Publishing, contact our
Business Development Team at
salesenquiries@murdochbooks.com.au.

Publisher: Jane Morrow
Editorial Managers: Katie Bosher and Julie Mazur Tribe
Design Manager: Vivien Valk
Illustrator: Alissa Dinallo
Project Editor: Shan Wolody
Photographer: Alan Benson
Stylist: Katy Holder
Home Economists: Grace Campbell and Wendy Quisumbing
Production Director: Lou Playfair

Recipes on the following pages appeared in *Whole Food Slow Cooked*
by Olivia Andrews, with photography by Steve Brown and styling by
Kristine Duran-Thiessen: 30, 37, 48–49, 52, 82, 86, 94, 102, 111, 161,
175, 183, 200.

A cataloguing-in-publication entry is available from the catalogue
of the National Library of Australia at nla.gov.au.

ISBN 978 1 76052 358 9 Australia
ISBN 978 1 76063 456 8 UK

A catalogue record for this book is available from the British Library.

Colour reproduction by Splitting Image Colour Studio Pty Ltd,
Clayton, Victoria
Printed by C & C Offset Printing Co. Ltd., China

The paper in this book is FSC®certified. FSC® promotes
environmentally responsible, socially beneficial and
economically viable management of the world's forests.

Acknowledgements

Thank you to Mud Australia and Studio Enti for
the loan of their gorgeous ceramics for the recipe
shoot. Thanks also to Olivia Andrews and to the
Murdoch test kitchen recipe writers for contributing
several recipes to this book.

Finally, thank you to the great photography team
of Alan Benson, Grace Campbell and Wendy
Quisumbing. Never have I seen so many slow
cookers in action at one time. Thanks for the
fun times.

—Katy Holder

IMPORTANT: Those who might be at risk from the
effects of salmonella poisoning (the elderly, pregnant
women, young children and those suffering from
immune deficiency diseases) should consult their
doctor with any concerns about eating raw eggs.

OVEN GUIDE: You may find cooking times vary
depending on the oven you are using. For fan-forced
ovens, as a general rule, set the oven temperature to
20°C (70°F) lower than indicated in the recipe.

MEASURES GUIDE: We have used 20 ml (4 teaspoon)
tablespoon measures. If you are using a 15 ml
(3 teaspoon) tablespoon add an extra teaspoon of
the ingredient for each tablespoon specified.